# BOXING

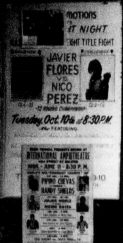

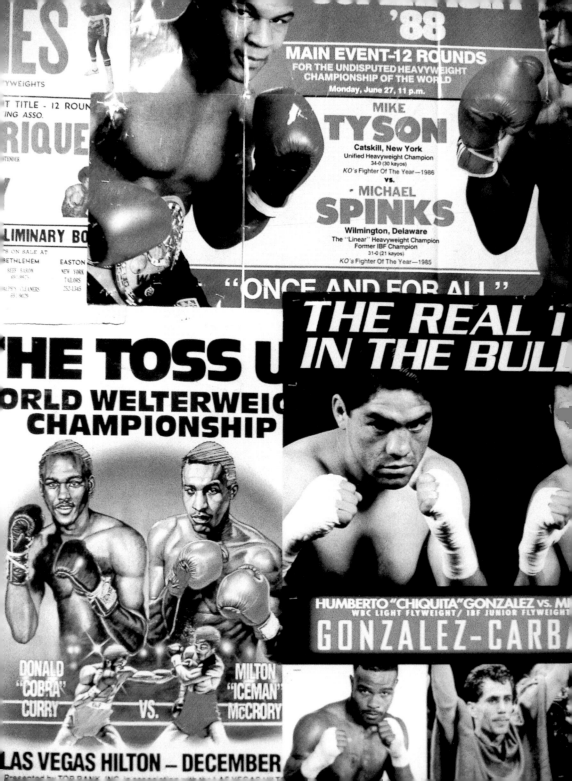

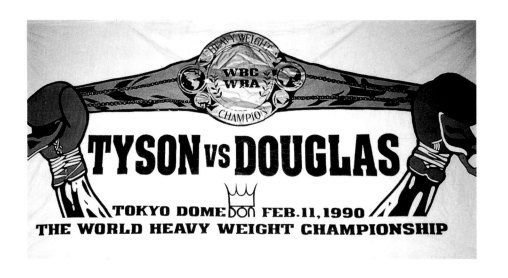

TYSON vs DOUGLAS
TOKYO DOME on FEB. 11, 1990
THE WORLD HEAVY WEIGHT CHAMPIONSHIP

© ASSOULINE, 1997
First published in France by Éditions Assouline, 1996

First published in the USA by UNIVERSE PUBLISHING
A Division of Rizzoli International Publications, Inc.
300 Park Avenue South, New York, NY 10010

English edition revised and updated
All Rights Reserved. No part of this publication may be reproduced,
stored in a retrieval system, or transmitted in any form or by any means, electronic,
mechanical, photocopying, recording, or otherwise, without prior consent of the publishers

ISBN 0-7893-0106-7

Library of Congress Catalog Card Number: 97-61192

Design: Olivier Assouline
Translated from the French by Sarah Creider
Copy editing: Chanterelle Translations, London
Typesetting: Studio X-Act.
Photo-engraving by Gravor, Switzerland.
Printed and bound in Hong Kong

# BOXING

PHOTOGRAPHS BY RICHARD AUJARD

TEXT BY CHRISTIAN DELCOURT

**WITH A PREFACE BY DON KING**

UNIVERSE

# CONTENTS

# DON KING

## PREFACE

**World Champion.** That's a title as strong as a right hook. It's the ultimate KO. To be given the title "World Champion" is to be recognized by the world as being capable of beating anyone, anywhere on the whole planet. The World Champion is simply the strongest man in his division. But these days, there are men who are even stronger: Unified World Champions. No one is more powerful. There's nothing higher. Unified champions dominate everyone. To arrive at the top of the pyramid requires an iron will and total concentration on a single objective—to be the best. A World Champion is also a man with a big heart, someone who gives it all he's got both in the ring and in training. A champion never thinks about defeat—only victory. And victory requires a lot from a man. He has to go beyond his limits and have a strong will, stronger than anyone else's. To reign as champion and to stay there for as long as possible is a daily battle. **You must prove yourself over and over again—forever.**

# J-C BOUTTIER

## FOREWORD

**Since time immemorial, young people have looked to role models, in every endeavor and at every level of life.** Regional champion, national champion, continental champion, World Champion. These days, the title "World Champion" is almost commonplace. And it has become even more so with the creation of each new federation (WBC, WBA, IBF, WBO). In the old days, there were only eight World Champions. Without years of training and hundreds of preliminary fights, you didn't stand a chance of becoming a star. Finally, you got the long-awaited opportunity to find yourself in a match against the man who was, unquestionably, the best in the division. Compare that to the way things are now: there are sixty-eight World Champions, seventeen divisions, and four federations. It's as if each title is shared four ways, like quarters of a title. Unified champions have become the exception that prove the rule in the boxing business. It's the era of boxing as show-biz. That's what the promoters and television sponsors want, and they have the power. But there is growing frustration everywhere: old-timers see the Noble Art turning its back on the principles for which they fought. Today's boxers find themselves propelled into championship matches long before they're ready, sometimes with only a few fights under their belts. Boxing aficionados are disappointed by the mediocre quality of many fights, and the general public is just plain confused. As the ranks of pugilists grow thinner, the number of champions continues to multiply. And yet, happily, the tradition of great and true champions continues. But are the best of today better or worse than the greats of the past? Could Holyfield have beaten Ali? Would Hagler have destroyed Roy Jones? Such comparisons are infinite, and infinitely unrealistic. Why live in the past? Things are the way they are, and it's easier today for young boxers to breech the ramparts of the inner circle of boxing. It's easier today to become one of many champions. But one thing is certain: **the best will always be the best. Champions will always be discovered. It's their destiny, no matter when they fight. The signs of greatness are unmistakable.**

# INTRODUCTION

**Is there a boxer anywhere who hasn't dreamed of one day experiencing the "nirvana of the Sweet Science?"** It is that supreme state, when a single golden punch plunges you into another universe—the universe of World Champions. Is there a man who isn't in awe of the valor, the courage, the determination, the physical force, the mental power, the conviction, even the faith of those who have gone beyond the limit, those who are in that "other" place? These two questions concern a myth: the myth of the "World Champion." The men who incarnate that myth embody the power of nature itself. They aspire to invulnerability and think of themselves as indestructible, unbeatable. They symbolize human vanity and human nobility at the same time. But the "law of the ring" is always there to bring this beautiful world back to cold, hard reality. Boxing is not a world for the innocent or pious, because with boxing, in a single flash of lightning, everything can be destroyed. In boxing, an entire life is sacrificed between four ropes, offered to the gods of boxing. And then these supermen quickly become just like the rest of us: simple human beings, with all the strengths of human beings, and, of course, all the weaknesses. To be a boxer is to accept this challenge, to follow an untrodden path. To risk honor, health, and even life itself. The sacrifice is almost inhuman. It's hard for mere mortals to understand. For many boxers, beyond all the pain and suffering lies the hope for a better life, a way out of poverty or a life of crime. It offers them the possibility "to be somebody," both professionally and financially. And for that, these men will do anything—as will the bigger world of the boxing business. Thanks to the impact of televised fights, the boxing business has become show business. Guided by untold millions of dollars, the Noble Art has transformed itself into a world of illusion. As a result, partially because of unified champions, the myth of the World Champion has grown at the same time that it's been debased. In the place of single champions, we have many. Federations and divisions are being created at the drop of a hat. World champions are multiplying faster than the blink of an eye. Today, there are sixty-eight boxers who have the right to the title. Compare that to only eight, as recently as the 1970s. If a boxer possesses a title, it's no longer a given that he has the talent to go with it. Are they real champions? Not always. As the divisions—from strawweight (105 lbs.) to heavyweight (the king of kings)—multiply, hoaxes and swindles become increasingly common. Even so, these fighters deserve nothing but respect. He who climbs into the ring knows the price. The joys, the dramas, the simple fact that at any moment a boxer could be catapulted into planet-wide fame— or receive the final blow, the one that will knock him out for good. Only boxing offers such moments of power and pain, just like those which the men presented in this book have lived through. **From Foreman to Tyson, and all the way to De la Hoya, these champions' histories will bring to you the real sensations of life in the ring. These are champions with heart, men in search of their own private truths. Emotion, violence, grandeur—this is the air breathed by World Champions.**

**PRAY FOR HIM**

*Vincent Pettway's prayers don't work this time. He's knocked-out by Paul Vaden. (August 1995)*

# HIST**ORY**

## *The legacy of the greats*

Even in boxing's early days, it was the heavyweights who got all the attention. Almost exactly one hundred years ago, as the nineteenth century drew to a close, a heavyweight distinguished himself and became one of the Sweet Science's first celebrities. **John Sullivan**, an Irish immigrant from Boston, proved you didn't have to count on the power of your fists alone in order to make it big in the ring. Sullivan, whose mother wanted him to be a pastor, was known to be quite a lady-killer. He would be the **first of the great American pros to make use of publicity**. By giving his personality a Hollywood-like dimension, he converted all his matches, from America to Europe, into big bucks. During his ten-year reign, from 1882 to 1892, Sullivan fought anyone who dared to challenge him—as long as they were white. Hate and fear have never been strangers.

**BARE FISTS**

*The noble art of boxing in the days of open-air matches. (late nineteenth century)*

At the turn of the century, under the initiative of the Marquess of Queensberry, fighting became a more humane sport. **By 1891, his new rules were being followed.** Three weight divisions were created. Lightweights had to be under 140 lbs., middleweights could weigh up to 154 lbs., and anyone over 154 lbs. qualified as a heavyweight. Rounds were limited to three minutes, separated by one minute of rest. Most important, gloves became mandatory. On September 7, 1892, in New Orleans, James Corbett's twenty-first round KO against John Sullivan heralded the end of an era. The Irishman, by this time an American idol, went on to follow his mother's wishes that he become a pastor. With Corbett (a former commissioner) on the scene, the modern era of Queensberry boxing made its triumphant debut. Boxing with gloves had nothing in common with the half-boxing/half-fighting tolerated under the old London rules. The heavyweight division was already showing signs of its destiny—to incite enormous interest, and to give birth to some of the twentieth century's most legendary champions.

## Jack Johnson
### first black heavyweight champion

On December 6, 1908, Sydney hosted the first World Heavyweight Championship between a black boxer, Jack Johnson, and a white boxer, Tommy Burns. Burns was fighting his thirteenth consecutive championship bout. Until then, he'd always avoided facing Johnson or any black boxer. Maybe he knew that after only a few rounds, Johnson's superior pugilistic style would make itself apparent. With the advantage of an impressive physique, Johnson overcame Burns in the fourteenth round, and won approximately $30,000. **With this victory, Jack Johnson, who only a few years earlier had labored in cotton fields, gave hope to millions of young black men.** It was the first time in the history of boxing that a black man gained the title of World Champion, and the news spread across America like wildfire.

Controversy erupted. Writer Jack London started a campaign against Johnson. He was searching for a "great white hope" who was capable of wiping what he deemed "the insolent smile of success" off the face of this first black Heavyweight Champion. Ex-

**FIRST BLACK CHAMPION**

*Jack Johnson—along with his punch, his range, and his iron will—meets Tommy Burns at the World Championship fight in Sydney. (December 1908)*

Middleweight Champion Stanley Ketchel, nicknamed "The Michigan Assassin," came out of retirement. A few extra pounds heavier than Johnson, he would come close to pulling it off. He knocked Johnson to the canvas in the second round. But as soon as Johnson got back up, he retaliated—with a KO. **The search for a white champion continued, while the hatred mounted.** Finally, Johnson was thrown out of U.S. boxing. He was charged with sleeping with white women, and his title was taken from him. Johnson moved to Europe, where he became World Champion again in Paris in 1913. He lost that title a few years later in Havana to Jesse Willard, who took the championship in the twenty-sixth round. Jack Johnson would continue to box until he was forty-nine, retiring with a total of one hundred and nine fights on his list of victories. But his biggest victory remains opening the door to other great black fighters.

## *Jack Dempsey, boxing's first real star*

Boxing has been the sport of some of the twentieth century's finest athletes. It has also been a shortcut to stardom for some of its champions. And the sport's first real celebrity was unquestionably the American Jack Dempsey. Dempsey was only twenty-four years old when his dreams came true. On July 4, 1919, he sent Jesse Willard to the canvas seven times, and this was only in the first round of their now legendary match-up. Saved by the bell, Willard managed to struggle through two more rounds before he gave up the ghost in round three.

**The golden age of boxing had begun.**
Frenchman George Carpentier arrived in Jersey City in 1921. He was ready to take up the challenge and take on Dempsey. Carpentier, basking in the glory of the World Middleweight Championship title, also had the aura of a star. **Eighty-thousand spectators** were present for the outdoor fight. **For the first time ever, the box office totals for the match, known as "the battle of the century," came to more than one million dollars: $1,789,238 to be exact.**
Carpentier, a national hero in France, was KO'd in the fourth round. Dempsey became a worldwide celebrity.
Philadelphia's Sesquicentennial Stadium hosted a crowd of record-breaking propor-

tions on September 23, 1926. Some one hundred twenty thousand fans came out to support their heroes, despite the rainy weather, which made for a very slippery ring. Gene Tunney turned Dempsey not only into a shadow of his former self, but into an object of ridicule. Two recent shake-ups in Dempsey's life—marriage to actress Estelle Taylor and giving his manager the boot—may have contributed to his reversal of fortune.

On September 22, 1927, the fans arrived at Soldier's Field in Chicago for a rematch. Dempsey knocked Tunney off his feet, but the count was too slow. The younger man was saved by a technicality. Dempsey lost by decision—an inglorious end for boxing's first real star.

### GENTLEMEN FIGHTERS

*Jack Dempsey and Gene Tunney pose for posterity*
*More than one hundred twenty thousand spectators are present for their confrontation. (September 1926)*

# *Joe Louis, the brown bomber*

June 22, 1937, was the beginning of the longest reign in the history of the heavyweight title. The record, which is for eleven years and three days, belongs to Joe Louis. With twenty-six consecutive World Championship fights, twenty-three won by KO or TKO, "the black bombardier" made boxing history. His record remains unbeaten to this day. Only the Mexican fighter, Julio Cesar Chavez, has come close. But Chavez's twenty-third championship fight, against Pernell Whitaker on September 10, 1993, finished as a draw. Within the ring, Joe Louis embodied the ideal of a great champion. Graceful, yet devastatingly ferocious, he showed his adversaries no mercy. "One day, this boy will accomplish great things with his hands," predicted one if Louis' primary school teachers.

Joe Louis' most famous fight took place in 1938. Facing him in the ring was the "Nazi hope," Max Schmeling, from Germany. Eighty-five thousand fans were there to support the American, who wanted to redeem himself for an earlier loss. In two minutes and four seconds, Joe Louis blasted the German, and pocketed $349,288. Or $2,816 a second. The legend of Joe Louis had just been born. The legend finally faded ten years later. After a loss

to Jersey Joe Walcott, the thirty-four-year-old Louis decided to give up his title. **His lifetime winnings totaled $4,626,721—one million of which went to the IRS for taxes.** Even so, Joe Louis shouldn't have had to worry about his retirement. But within a few years, a series of bad investments and a taste for the high life left him almost penniless. The world outside the ring was a "fight" for which Joe Louis didn't seem to have trained.

**LITTLE JOE TURNS INTO A BIG FIGHTER**

*Joe Louis still holds the record for consecutive World Championships: twenty-six titles between 1937 and 1948.*

*Rocky Marciano,*
*greatest white heavyweight*
*of all time*

**Rocky Marciano, the man who would become a legend,** was born on September 1, 1923, in Philadelphia. After Joe Louis' retirement, the division of kings waited for a new sovereign. Despite nine championships and a victory over Louis, Ezzard Charles just wasn't convincing. Neither was Jersey Joe Walcott. But it was against Walcott, with a thirteenth round KO, that Marciano showed the qualities and courage that would make him champion. This success which was confirmed nine months later against the same man, with another KO—this time in the first round. Considered quiet and timid in his daily life, Rocky, once in the ring, **became a machine of destruction, as inexorable as a bulldozer.**

An ex-GI, he had discovered boxing while in the army. On his return from Cardiff, where he had been stationed during World War II, he immediately engaged in his first professional fights. He eventually defended his title six times, fighting against some of boxing's greatest, if also somewhat aging men, like Ezzard Charles (thirty-three), Joe Louis (thirty-seven), Jersey Joe Walcott (thirty-eight), and Archie Moore (forty). It was the time of the "little heavyweights," where men who didn't weigh much more than 195 lbs. still possessed surprising power to go with their mobility and rapidity. For four years, Marciano occupied the throne of his generation, until he retired, unique among heavyweight champions, with a perfect record after forty-nine fights. **"I saw that my face was starting to get deformed. It didn't deserve that."** Provided with a comfortable fortune, he didn't have long to enjoy the ease that his fearlessness and skill had given him. In 1969, he died when his private plane crashed, and was mourned above all by the great black boxers of his generation. **He remains the greatest white heavyweight in the history of boxing.**

# Muhammad Ali
## champion of the century

In Miami, on February 25, 1962, the odds were seven-to-one against Cassius Clay as he prepared to fight Sonny Liston, the World Champion at the time. Clay, crowned Olympic Heavyweight Champion two years earlier, started his boxing career in 1954 in Louisville, when he came running into a boxing gym in tears. **He told the trainer someone had stolen his bicycle, and asked for help in catching the thief. The trainer suggested to young Cassius that if he learned how to box he would be able to fight his own battles.** Before his first fight, Clay began a tradition that would continue throughout his career; he predicted the round that he would win, on this occasion in the eighth. But he underestimated his powers. When the seventh round was called, Liston remained in his corner, prostrate with an injury. Quite simply, the champion of the century had arrived.

**"I am the greatest, and I'm only twenty-two."** Ali planned to stick around for a long time. Just before climbing into the ring to take on Liston, Clay had converted to Islam and, therefore, had decided to leave his "slave name" behind and engaged in another fight: the battle for African-Americans to thwart racism in American society.

Ali defended his title for nine years straight. Then, in 1967, a low blow took the title away from him. Politically opposed to the Vietnam War, Ali refused to join the army. "I don't see why a black man should kill a yellow man for the sake of a white man," he argued. Forbidden by the draft board to fight for three years, he was finally allowed to return to the ring in 1970. **Likening the heavyweights who had held "his" throne during his absence to "trash," he announced that he was still the most beautiful and the best.** In 1971, the "fight of the century" pit Ali against Joe Frazier, champion since Ali's suspension from the ring. But was Ali still the artist, the "dancer, puncher, hitter" of his early days? He was certainly sure of himself. "To beat me, you have to be a great champion. If Frazier beats me, that means he's a great champion." Perhaps Ali was too confident. He had forgotten that this was only his third fight since he returned from his forced "retirement." It was not enough. Madison Square Garden in New York hosted the first match in history where two undefeated heavyweight champions went up against each other. The historic occasion was nothing but disaster for Ali. His confidence was shattered. In the fifteenth round he was on the ground, and for the first time ever he lost a match by decision—unanimously. The crowd, most of them against Ali because of his "desertion" during the war, exalted. Frazier's victory was complete. The premier division began a golden age, with four "greats" to its name: Frazier, Foreman, Norton, and Ali. Ali, beaten once again by Norton, saw Frazier lose his title to Foreman. But the era of boxing as a business had begun—and thus so did the rematches. Ali revenged his defeat against Norton, and proceeded to take on Frazier, again at Madison Square Garden in New York, on January 28, 1974. Twenty-thousand spectators were present, **and the fight brought in an unprecedented total of thirty-five million dollars (including twenty-five million from television rights)** for a match with no title at stake. A sobered Ali exerted himself, managing to win. But he didn't really dominate the fight. And Frazier was no longer the champion he once was. Indeed, after his first confrontation with Ali, the man known as "Smokin' Joe" had spent twelve days in the hospital. Two years later, Frazier would lose his title to George box Foreman in less than two rounds, after finding himself on the canvas six times.

For Ali, winner by decision, the road to the

### THE LOOK OF A FUTURE CHAMPION

*At thirteen, Cassius Clay already has his eyes on the prize.*

World Championship was once again clear. On November 30, 1974, the world watched as Don King promoted his first World Championship, in Kinshasa, Zaire: **"The rumble in the jungle," Ali vs. George Foreman.** Ali was a three-to-one favorite, in front of sixty-two thousand spectators. "I'm gonna beat his Christian behind, white man with his little flag," said Ali, who hadn't appreciated the patriotism of Foreman, who waved a little American flag after winning the '68 Olympic gold medal in Mexico City. He empathized more with the black sprinters like John Carlos and Tommy Smith, who punched black-gloved fists into the air as they stood on the Olympic victory podium, symbolizing their support for the Black Power movement. After just a few days in Africa, Ali had become a beloved if self-appointed spokesman for blacks everywhere. It seemed as if the entire African continent, including Zaire's President Mobutu, was behind him.

"Al-lee booma ya." Everywhere Ali went, he heard his fans chanting, **"Ali, kill him."** He knew what all the noise was about. And with so many people behind him, he knocked out Foreman in the eighth round. Ali joined Floyd Patterson as one of only two heavyweights to have regained the ultimate title. **"This evening it's not Ali who KO'd Foreman. No, it's Allah himself, incarnated in me, because you all know that I don't have the punch."** Divine or physical force, one thing was certain—Ali and Foreman each earned five million dollars for the match. Before the fight in Zaire, Ali had talked about retiring from boxing. After, he changed his mind. The sweet sensations of victory were hard to leave behind. And the easy money he could earn fighting against unknowns was irresistible. The "Ali circus" was a bonanza, especially promoted heavily on television. Each match brought out between thirty-three and fifty million television viewers in the U.S. One minute of commercials during one of his televised matches was worth one hundred twenty thousand dollars. Ali was always a draw. He himself said he would box anywhere, even on the moon, as long as he earned enough money.

On December 1, 1975, in Manila, Ali and Frazier met up once again. "I'll kill the gorilla," shouted Ali, hammering his fists against a little statue of a gorilla in his hands. Another name for Joe Frazier Ali loved to use was the "lout." Frazier had beaten his opponents one after another with the same unrelenting, monotonous rhythm, without style or originality. The "Thrilla in Manila" ended with the annihilation of Frazier. Both men were exhausted, but Frazier was really running on empty, his face heavily swollen from taking Ali's precision hits. The ring doctor and Frazier's trainer, Eddie Futch, decided to stop the third and final combat between the two men. "From now on, there's no question that Joe Frazier is the best boxer in history—after me." Always ready with a well-turned phrase, Ali later said that he had been ready to give up the fight in the tenth round. His success continued. But then, on February 15, 1978, after another "beautiful" victory against Norton, Ali met Leon Spinks. The fight took place in Las Vegas, and Spinks, an Olympic champion in 1976, won by decision. The great champion was getting tired, exemplifying the difference between a man who's spent his entire life being battered in the ring and one fighting in only his eighth professional match. The tide was turning, the end drawing near. Seven months later, Ali took back his title, with difficulty, but achieving a record that he still holds: to be the only boxer to win back his title three times. The hour of farewell had finally arrived. Despite his waning powers, he picked one fight too many two years later. The thirty-nine-year-old Ali fought Larry Holmes, but finally threw in the towel after eleven rounds. It was the end of the greatest of the greats. Stricken with Parkinson's disease in recent years, Ali is active still and remains an enormously courageous and inspirational figure to all Americans.

## *The end of an era*

In the 1970s, anarchy overtook the heavyweight division. Now that Ali was out of the picture, the once glorious title found itself contested again. In 1962, the World Boxing Association (WBA) had been created, and by 1978 the first fractures began to appear. Leon Spinks refused to fight his official challenger, Ken Norton, preferring a more lucrative rematch against Ali. Spinks therefore was stripped of the unified title, keeping only the WBA crown, while Norton became the Heavyweight Champion of the WBC, the World Boxing Council. With the creation, in 1982, of the International Boxing Federation (IBF), true chaos began. Boxers could only dream of a third of a title. Or of a fourth, after the WBO, the World Boxing Organization, was created in 1988. During the early eighties, confusion reigned. But promoter Don King **succeeded in reunifying the supreme title. His fighter was Mike Tyson.** Tyson's reign only lasted three years, from 1987 to 1990. Tyson was incarcerated in 1990 for a felony, and anarchy got the upper hand again.

# L'ÉQUIPE
## LE QUOTIDIEN · 8 pages · DU SPORT

## GRANDE CARRIÈRE TOUTE SIMPLE

*Il était un homme follement populaire, un père tendre, un ami affectueux*

### De l'angoisse au dra...

### Il était la vie

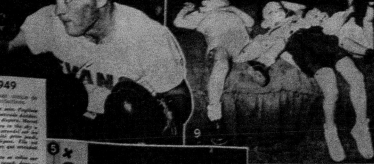

1929—1949

# The middleweight stars:
## Cerdan, Graziano, La Motta, Zale

In addition to the heavyweight category, other divisions have flourished through the years. Today, from strawweights to heavyweights, there are a total of seventeen weight divisions. Of the "lesser" divisions, it's the middleweights (160 lbs.) who have provided the most memorable champions. At the beginning of this century, men like the American **Stanley Ketchel** or the Frenchman **Marcel Thil** were paving the way for the next generation of stars. But it was not until the 1940s that the era of great middleweight champions truly began. Americans **Tony Zale, Rocky Graziano,** and **Jack La Motta** were soon joined by welterweight **Sugar Ray Robinson** and the famous Frenchman **Marcel Cerdan**. Zale was the first grand champion of these glorious years. His combat against Rocky Graziano in three matchups is still remembered by many boxing aficionados.

In 1948, Zale met the "Moroccan Bombardier," Marcel Cerdan. Twelve rounds later, Zale, KO'd, retired from the ring, his last fight ending in defeat. Worried about regaining the title as soon as possible, American promoters immediately found a challenger. In 1949, in Detroit, La Motta took back the title in the eleventh round. Then disaster struck. On October 27, 1949, Marcel Cerdan left Paris for the United States, hoping to take the title back from La Motta. Cerdan's plane, an Air France Constellation, crashed into the peak of Mount Redondo in the Azores. **The loss of France's greatest boxer was a tragedy mourned throughout the boxing world.**

# From Robinson
## to Monzon

As the 1950s began, La Motta's career came to an end and Sugar Ray Robinson took his place among the ranks of the middleweight stars. Robinson, who had already won the Welterweight title six times between 1946 and 1950, was hardly a boxing neophyte. When he sent La Motta to the canvas in the thirteenth round, Sugar Ray gave the final blow to one middleweight's career, and began another—his own phenomenal era. **Sugar Ray Robinson spent twenty-five years of his life in the ring. He fought in**

**202 matches, won 175 of them, 109 times by KO, and lost only nineteen times, with six draws, and two no contests.** Remarkably, he won the Middleweight title five times during the '50s. **In the ring, he is said to have danced like Fred Astaire and to have possessed the elegance of the Great Gatsby.**

After Robinson, making a name for oneself wasn't easy. Another American, Emil Griffith, and the Italian Nino Benvenuti, provided three memorable meetings in New York during the latter half of the '60s, but **it was only Carlos Monzon who could stake a real claim for the mantle of Robinson.** The "Argentine Bull" would bring every one of his adversaries to their knees, dominating his division between 1970 and 1977. When he finally retired, he had claimed fifteen victorious championship matches. Among his accomplishments were two fights each against the best fighters of his generation: Nino Benvenuti, Emile Griffith, Jean-Claude Bouttier, Benny Briscoe, and Rodrigo Valdez.

## The wonder years: Hagler, Hearns, Leonard, and Duran

**While Marvin Hagler began** his domination of the '80s with a fight in London, it was in the U.S. that the American became "Marvelous" (the name he now uses on his passport). From 1980 to 1987, Hagler was at the top of a division that contained three other great champions: Roberto Duran, Thomas Hearns, and Sugar Ray Leonard.

In the '80s, Las Vegas traded in its title as Capital of Betting and became the Capital of Boxing. The casinos came to blows in the contest for the flashiest boxing posters. In 1983, Hagler beat Duran, and, in 1985, he demolished Hearns with a KO in the thirteenth round of one of the greatest fights in history. Two years later, in his thirteenth championship, after eleven years of invincibility, Hagler was outpointed by "Leonard the artist." **Leonard had predicted that he'd beat the boxer's style, not the man himself.**

**LEONARD THE ARTIST**

*When he's in the ring, boxing becomes magic. (1976–1991)*

Sugar Ray had had to spend five years away from the ring recovering from a detached retina. Now back, he had two goals: to beat Hagler, and to retire once again. Disheartened, thinking he'd been wronged, it was Hagler who retired for good, giving up the millions of dollars which were up for grabs by the end of the decade.

After his remarkable success, Leonard tried for a second come-back nineteen months later. The man who had already taken three titles in the welterweight, junior middleweight, and middleweight divisions was on a quest for posterity. On November 7, 1988, he won the WBC Super Middleweight and Light Heavyweight titles in one blow, beating Don Lalonde.

**With five titles in five different divisions, Sugar Ray Leonard moved into the ranks of "God of the ring."** Three days later, another boxer won his fifth division title. Thomas Hearns walked off with the WBO Super Middleweight crown, having already won titles in the welterweight, junior middleweight, light heavyweight, and middleweight divisions. The two quintuple champions met for a match in 1989 that was simply titled, **"The War."**

Unfortunately, the greatly hyped-up fight offered only a few chance moments of genius. The "old soldiers" (Leonard was thirty-three and Hearns thirty-one) had been in too many matches since their professional debuts in 1977, and the fight ended as a draw.

By that time, Leonard had won eleven million dollars against Hagler, twelve million against Lalonde, and thirteen million against Hearns. For his last legendary combat, he took on Duran, on December 7, 1989. The American had already met the Panamanian twice, and Duran was the only man to have beaten the unbeatable Leonard (in 1980, as a welterweight). This time, Leonard got his revenge with no problem.

Fourteen months later, Sugar Ray Leonard, beaten by Terry Norris at Madison Square Garden in New York, finally left the ring for good. With another five million dollars, his winnings come close to the hundred million dollar mark, earned during fourteen years of magnificent combat. **Like his namesake, Sugar Ray Robinson, Leonard remains a giant in the history of boxing's greats.**

# Champions from every division

**Almost all of boxing's stars come from the two most prestigious divisions: heavyweight and middleweight.** Who remembers Manual Ortiz, World Bantamweight Champion from 1942 to 1949? Or what about any one of Eusebio Pedroza's twenty successes as WBA Featherweight Champion from 1978 to 1985? Who could cite even one of the twenty boxers beaten by World Welterweight Champion Henry Armstrong during only twenty-eight months, between 1938 and 1940? With the proliferation of federations and the growing number of divisions, boxing has changed considerably in recent years.

**Unified champions no longer exist. Instead we have "quarter champions." Except for Mike Tyson, it has been more than a decade since any boxer has succeeded in reunifying the titles.** The role of television promoters, the federations, the importance of image and of television contracts, all have moved boxing in another direction. But a unified champion would certainly give boxing some much-needed credibility. Imagine a super champion in each division, with an additional belt. The dreams of champions are limitless.

In a world where titles garner enormous respect, the men who hold them have star billings. Whether they stay at the top for an eternity, the length of a decade, or for a few fights, before falling once again into anonymity, their names, alongside the title World Champion, will always be written into boxing history. **Even if the dream is behind them, the respect remains.**

# WORLD CHAMPIONS:

## FROM TYSON TO DE LA HOYA

**There are no easy truths in boxing—** or, at least, precious few of them. With a decisive uppercut, a crushing hook, or a percussive jab, a career is either born or it see-saws between the bright lights of the ring and the shadows of failure. From Mike Tyson to Oscar De la Hoya, each of the eighteen champions presented here has quite a history. They embody everything the world of boxing has to offer at the end of the twentieth century. As living gods of the ring and stars of the media, they're already the stuff of legend. Thanks to televised broadcasts of their fights, these men are known even in the most remote regions of the world. During a time of multiple champions, they have risen to the top. **They are all members of an exclusive club, where myths are created, and where respect is demanded.**

MIKE

# tyson

Youngest World Champion in boxing history

**HAND OF THE PROPHET**

*Converted to Islam while in prison, Mike Tyson is back in the ring (August 1995)*

**"I'm going to box again."** It was the phrase the boxing world had been waiting for ever since Mike Tyson was convicted of rape and imprisoned on March 25, 1992. Boxing wouldn't be the same during the three years "Big Brother" Tyson spent in jail. Tyson, who became a legend in 1987 as the only boxer to reunite the heavyweight title, proved to be irreplaceable. So, on March 25, 1995, in front of Indiana's state penitentiary, the press came out in droves to witness this unforgettable moment in boxing history, a pivotal instant that linked the past and the future. Number 922335 was once again a free man, a boxer. There was no doubt about it. Mike Tyson was back.

Tyson's announcement was made on March 30, in Cleveland, Ohio, just five days after his release. Since leaving prison, Tyson had only appeared in public for a few seconds at a time. During his press conference, he said he'd spent the last three years thinking about his life. Now he was ready to become a better man, and a better boxer. He insisted that, despite all the speculation on his future, he was determined to box again. Watch in hand, Tyson would speak for exactly one minute and two seconds—just long

**MIKE TYSON**

UNITED STATES

BORN JUNE 30, 1966

48 FIGHTS

45 WINS (39 BY KO)

3 LOSSES

WBC WORLD HEAVYWEIGHT
CHAMPION IN 1986
WBA-WBC WORLD HEAVY-
WEIGHT CHAMPION IN 1987
WBA-WBC-IBF WORLD
HEAVYWEIGHT CHAMPION
FROM 1987 TO 1990
WBA-WBC WORLD HEAVY-
WEIGHT CHAMPION IN 1996

enough to erase any last doubts. Boxing fans were KO'd with happiness.

Tyson fought for his first world title on November 22, 1986, against Trevor Berbick. Since his professional debut, the boxer from Brooklyn had been a quick worker, and this fight was no exception. By the second round, Berbick was annihilated, pulverized. He couldn't even raise himself to his knees. The ropes tossed him from one side of the ring to the other. This KO remains one of the most terrifying in recent years. The new WBC Heavyweight Champion of the world was the youngest champion in the history of heavyweights: twenty years, four months, and twenty-two days old. "Iron Mike" Tyson now faxed the challenge of following in the footsteps of his illustrious predecessors: Johnson, Louis, and Ali.

Tyson represents power in its most natural state. He is a force of nature with only one word in his head—"destroy." His rise to glory was lightning-quick. Christened the youngest unified champion, after his successes against James Smith (WBA title, March 7, 1987) and Tony Tucker (IBF title, August 1, 1987), he began, with his three belts, to seem invincible. And he was. He proved it against the best. Larry Holmes, for instance, thought he was going to pound some reason into young Tyson's head. But Holmes resisted for only four rounds. On January 22, 1988, he was pulverized by "Iron Mike." It was the same for Tony Tubbs, beaten in two rounds, and for Michael Spinks, unstoppable until then. General opinion had it that Spinks was one of the few boxers capable of beating Tyson, but he only lasted 91 seconds. Spinks "said hello to the stars" and ended his career on the canvas, KO'd. Another impressive victory for the young man who had no time to lose in the ring.

Master of the world, Tyson was a celebrity at the height of his powers. He had it all: fame, glory, money. What more could a boxer ask for? Then, in the beginning of 1990, his confidence received a big blow. In Tokyo, he faced James Buster Douglas.

The odds were forty-two to one against Buster at the betting booths. But during his press conference, the unknown challenger was strangely confident. Douglas said he'd been watching Tyson, and he wasn't impressed. He boasted that the unstoppable star was about to be stopped—by him. And he was right. It was the biggest upset in the history of boxing. Tyson was knocked out in the tenth round of his eleventh championship defense,

**EYE OF THE TIGER**

*The look in Tyson's eyes strikes fear into the hearts of his opponents. (1995)*

# TYSON IS
## A FORCE OF NATURE
## POWER IN ITS
## NATURAL STATE
### HE ONLY HAS ONE WORD IN HIS HEAD:
# DESTROY

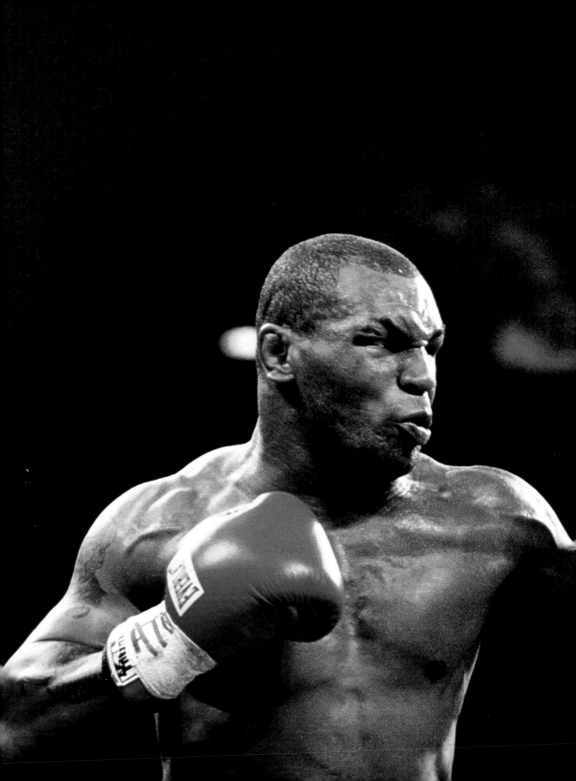

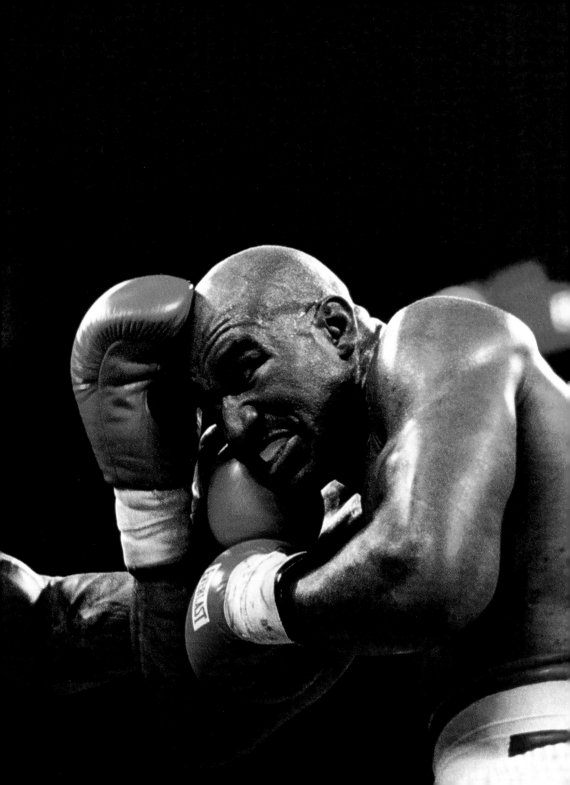

as Douglas proved himself to be a destroyer of myths and dreams. It was easy to lose, said Tyson after the fight, but only the best make it back to the top. The world began a long wait. The whole heavyweight division paid the price for Tyson's loss, and it fell into disarray a few years later. As for Tyson, he was headed for Indiana.

His return to the ring was planned for August 19, 1995. One thousand five hundred and five days after facing Donovan Ruddock during his last fight in June 1991. It was an eternity for a champion, and for the world of boxing. He would be more than four years away from the heady perfume of the ring. "I'm confident that I'm going to be the best again. Everyone always thought I was number one. And I don't see why that shouldn't continue. I'm back to reunify the title, and no one, absolutely no one is going to stand in my way. I'm hungry, and I'm only after one thing: victory." And, in August of 1995, the boxing world wanted to go back to "the Tyson years." The media was screaming "He's Back." The fever mounted. His entourage had predicted his victory. And, in fact, challenger Peter McNeeley's "day of glory" didn't last more than eighty-nine seconds at MGM Las Vegas. The match was so brief, Tyson hardly had the time to rediscover the sensations of World Championship boxing. He sent his mediocre opponent to the canvas twice, and the fight was finally stopped by McNeeley's manager in a controversial move. Tyson's return was disappointing, despite his efforts. Famous promoter Don King had orchestrated the champion's return, with the help of the fighter's two young managers, Rory Holloway and John Horne. Tyson's comeback earned him forty million dollars—a lot of money for a simple fight, with nothing at stake except satisfying a public hungry to see him in the ring once again.

By the time fight number two rolled around, Tyson was thinking about his future. This time, he had to face Buster Mathis Junior, on November 4, 1995. But a broken right thumb sent Tyson's already high level of frustration soaring. The fight was postponed to December 16, at Philadelphia. Tyson claimed he'd made progress in training, but, once again, the fight fell below expectations. His attacks were off for almost three rounds, until

### RETURN TO SUCCESS

(PRECEDING PAGES AND OPPOSITE) *Tyson vs Holyfield, 28 June 1997. "He's back!" In eighty-nine seconds and a few devastating punches, Tyson destroys McNeely (August 1995)*

(FOLLOWING PAGES) *Mike Tyson, sure of his power against Frank Bruno. The American took back the WBC World Championship in three quick rounds.*

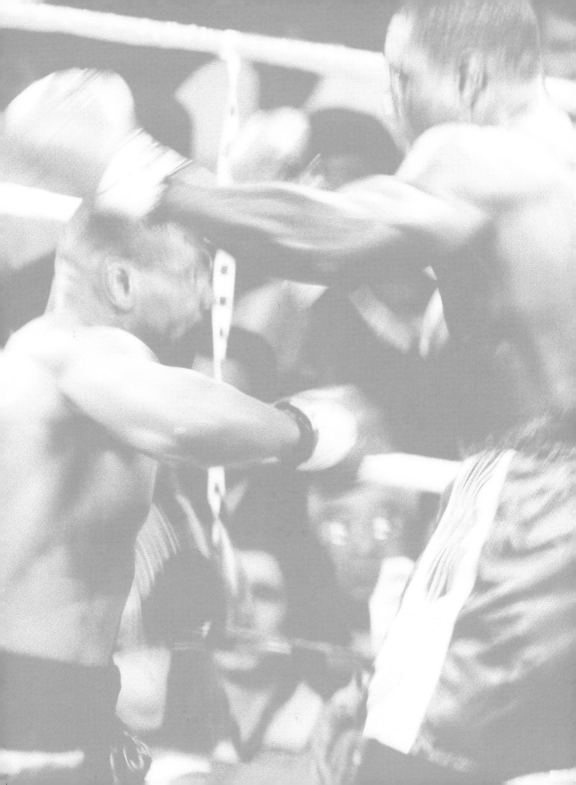

a punishing right uppercut reminded the world of how, with one blow, Mike Tyson could destroy anything.

After two fights (and only ten minutes and one second spent in the ring), Tyson had found his old style again. Tyson met Bruno in a WBC World Championship fight on March 16, 1996, at Las Vegas. This was the first real challenge of the year, a practice session before facing the WBA and IBF champions. Most boxing fans had no doubt that Tyson would once again destroy Britannic Bruno, and thus regain his place as World Champion. After all, the last time the two fighters met, on February 25, 1989, Bruno had been annihilated after five rounds. The fans were right. Seven years after that first match, "Iron Mike" exploded back onto the scene. The fight was over in less than three rounds. His opponent was simply outfought, incapable of offering a reply worthy of being called a challenge. In reality, Tyson was the winner before he even entered the ring. During the traditional pre-fight weigh-in, Bruno, even with the protection of his dark glasses, couldn't look the glowering Tyson in the eye.

The comeback, in three brief episodes, would earn Tyson twenty million dollars, for only sixteen minutes and fifty-one seconds spent in the ring. After his historic fight against Douglas, Tyson was so sure of himself, he didn't think he would ever be beaten again. He would be a legend for the end of the century. His first World Championship against Bruno was called "Championship: Part One." The future is in his hands.

After yet another championship fight postponed and a short fight against Bruce Seldon, who was petrified with fear before the combat, Tyson met Holyfield on November 9, 1996. "No one will ever beat me again," Tyson had declared after his historical defeat against Douglas. That night, however, Holyfield dominated Tyson both tactically and technically and Tyson was stopped by the referee in the eleventh round. The Tyson myth was shattered. And on June 28, 1997, the date of the most eagerly awaited revenge match in the history of boxing, the legend was utterly destroyed. In the third round Tyson bared his teeth and bit off part of Holyfield's right ear. Tyson effectively disqualified himself from the sport that had made him famous. Once again, his future looked dark, even though he had made 150 million dollars in winnings since his comeback.

OLOR SPECIAL #2
RFIGHT
88
2 ROUNDS
EAVYWEIGHT
HE WORLD
1 p.m.
ON
w York
ght Champion
yos)
e Year—1986
AEL
NKS
Delaware
weight Champion
Champion
kayos)
The Year—1985
FOR ALL"
REAL THI

# GEORGE

# foreman

Oldest heavyweight champion in boxing history

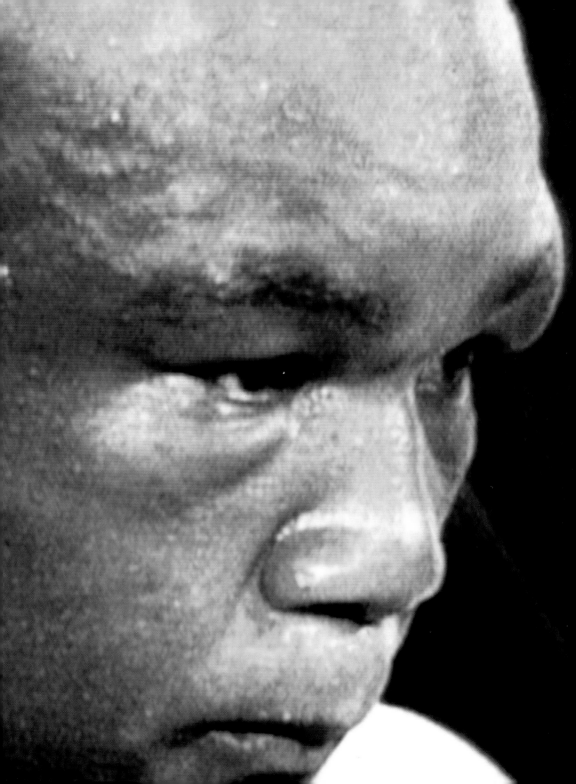

**THE SHOULDERS OF A CHAMPION**

*Inside the ring, George Foreman became a star. (November 1994)*

**It was November 5, 1994. The MGM Las Vegas, the world's largest hotel,** was taken over by the monotony of one more WBA-IBF Heavyweight Championship. Twenty-six-year-old Michael Moorer was the reigning champion. He was following the strict orders of his trainer, Teddy Atlas. Using his jab, dancing around the ring, Moorer had managed to avoid George Foreman's famous right hook. Foreman was attempting the impossible. Almost forty-six years old, "Big George" wanted to regain the world title, twenty years after he was first crowned champion in Kingston, on January 22, 1974.

Suddenly, Moorer, ahead by a large margin, forgot his instructions. He found himself facing Foreman head on. A straight left was followed by a right hook to the jaw. Moorer collapsed, and the crowd roared with pleasure as the referee counted: eight, nine, ten, out. It was nothing short of a miracle. On his knees, thanking God, "Big George" was in heaven. Born in Texas, Foreman had a difficult childhood. At a young age, he fell into a life of delinquency. But pride pulled him through. He joined a charitable self-help group, and took up boxing in 1967. "Finally, my first fight in a ring," he said, alluding to his street-fighting past. One year later, wielding a mighty combination of power and punch, he won the Olympic heavyweight title at the games in Mexico. After the match, he stirred up controversy by waving a tiny American flag in the ring, while other African-American athletes, most notably sprinters John Carlos and Tommy Smith, climbed onto the podium wearing black berets and waving their black-gloved fists in the air. Foreman was accused of treason in the fight for civil rights.

But when it came to the kind of fight he'd been training for, Foreman showed real promise. He turned pro and the KOs accumulated, but the sports writers only talked about the mediocrity of opponents. Finally, at the age of twenty-four, he had his first chance for a world title, in Kingston, Jamaica. He had thirty-eight victories, with thirty-five KOs, under his belt. Facing him was "Smokin'" Joe Frazier, fresh from fending off Ali's blows, and favored to win, with three-to-one odds. The odds didn't matter. Frazier lost in less than two rounds, after six trips to the canvas. Foreman delivered one uppercut that was so powerful it literally lifted Frazier off his feet. The referee finally stopped the fight, which had turned into a massacre. After defending his title in two matches as quick as the first one, against José Roman (KO in Round One) and Ken Norton (KO in Round Two), Foreman was finally defeated by Ali in Zaire, on October 30, 1974. Thirty-three-year-old Ali was full of pre-fight predictions. Worse, he continued to taunt Foreman in the ring, waging a battle more psychological than physical. He called Foreman a monster and said he hit like a girl. Foreman, used to quick victories, exhausted himself in the hot and humid Zairian night. In the eighth round, Ali's talent won over the brute force of "Big George," who was knocked down for the first time in his career.

To put himself back into circulation, Foreman began a new and somewhat bizarre training program. In Toronto, he took on, and beat, five boxers in one afternoon. His ego reassured, the big man threw himself into the battle to regain his title. It wasn't easy. In 1977, in San Juan, Puerto Rico, he lost by decision to Jimmy Young. Returning to his dressing room, Foreman collapsed. That's when things took an interesting turn. Thinking he had died, Foreman felt the spirit of Jesus enter his body. His entourage was persuaded that it was simply a case of exhaustion and heat stroke, but for Foreman, it was a revelation. He announced his retirement, and declared that although he had always recited from the Bible, he had never really read it. He talked about a newfound happiness. "Big George"

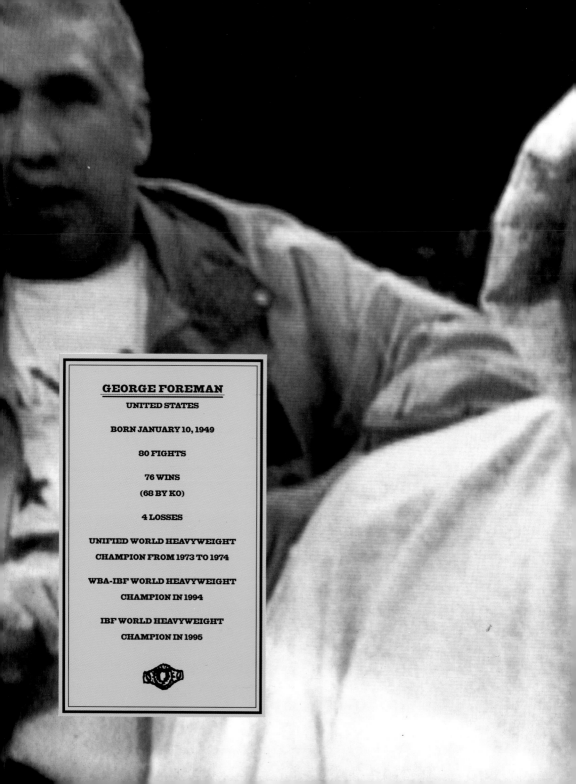

## GEORGE FOREMAN

### UNITED STATES

BORN JANUARY 10, 1949

80 FIGHTS

76 WINS

(68 BY KO)

4 LOSSES

UNIFIED WORLD HEAVYWEIGHT
CHAMPION FROM 1973 TO 1974

WBA-IBF WORLD HEAVYWEIGHT
CHAMPION IN 1994

IBF WORLD HEAVYWEIGHT
CHAMPION IN 1995

became the pastor of a tiny church, spending his free time with his seven children, five of whom are named George.

Ten years later, in 1987, a news flash shocked sports writers everywhere. "Foreman is coming back." The ex-champion wanted three things: money (a large portion of which was destined for charity), the world title, and Tyson. "Old George" had something to say to "Young Mike," now at the peak of his career. The specialists snickered, making jokes at Foreman's expense. But the fans were behind him. They wanted to see the Foreman phenomenon. Pot-bellied, bald, and slow, he still managed to crush his adversaries. Within the ring, this preacher was no saint.

The American press continued to laugh. They underlined the extreme weakness of Foreman's opponents, but they couldn't deny that he was a changed man. Gone was the boxer who once was so taciturn and unaccommodating with the press. In his place was a smiling grandfather. George Foreman had found inner peace. He spread laughter everywhere he went, spouting jokes and witticisms. The public was entranced. And "Big George" lined up victory after victory—twenty-four in a row, twenty-three by KO.

On April 19th, Foreman received twelve million dollars, offered for fighting the World Champion, Evander Holyfield. Twenty-eight years old, Holyfield weighed only 210 lbs., while Foreman boasted 250 lbs. "It's my trump card," said Foreman, perfectly seriously. He claims that a high-powered diet (which includes eating bacon and up to twelve eggs for breakfast) gives him enough reserves to keep on fighting when other boxers would already have fallen to the wayside, exhausted.

"The Shock of the Generations" brought twenty thousand fans to Atlantic City's Convention Center, while a record one-and-a-half million Americans took advantage of cable's "Pay-per-view" to watch the match in their own living rooms. Foreman didn't have the footwork he used to, a definite disadvantage. Holyfield unleashed a series of twenty blows. He ran Foreman's old legs all over the ring, but the "Dinosaur" resisted. In the end, Holyfield won by decision, while Foreman won something more important than any sin-

## A FORCE OF NATURE

(OPPOSITE) *"Big George" built his reputation on rough replies to hard questions,
on a training regime he follows religiously. But his reputation is nothing compared to the man himself,
as Axel Schulz and Michael Moorer learned for themselves.*

gle match: respect. At forty-two years old, he proved his credibility and continued down his chosen path, earning more than five million dollars per appearance. But, on June 17, 1993, Foreman slowed down when he lost a WBA world title match by decision to the "white hope," Tommy Morrison. This loss left the question of his retirement foremost in everyone's mind.

He answered the question with his historic win against Michael Moorer, a young boxer who Foreman said reminded him of one of his own sons. Foreman became the oldest World Champion ever, at forty-five years and ten months. "You can't beat a miracle. And I'm a miracle," he had declared before losing the fight against Holyfield. This time, the "miracle" really did happen. Even if Foreman had only fulfilled two of his three goals, he'd certainly filled up his bank account—with more than he ever could have expected.

On April 22, 1995, the forty-six-year-old Foreman, his WBA title taken from him for having refused to fight his official challenger, took on the modest German fighter Alex Schultz for the IBF title. But the weight of the years was too much for "Big George" and the victory was "given" to him. Refusing a rematch, Foreman preferred to forget about this last title, and concentrated his efforts on a farewell fight, scheduled for February 29, 1996, at Madison Square Garden in Manhattan. Facing Foreman was not Mike Tyson (for whom the box office totals would have exceeded twenty million dollars) but Michael Moorer. A rematch with a ten million dollar purse. But the fight never took place. HBO, who had scheduled to televise "Big George's" last match, wanted to pay Foreman's huge fee in installments because no one believed that he really planned on quitting.

Several months later he did climb back into the ring. For the glory? No. For the bucks. For his fight in April 1997 against Lou Savarese, Foreman pocketed four million dollars. The George Foreman myth still brought in big money, despite his rather unconvincing performances. So why stop? He says that he wants to keep on fighting until he's fifty. Secretly, "Preacher George" is still hoping to knock Tyson out one of these days. Meanwhile, his congregation prays that such a fight will never happen. "Dear God, don't let him fight one fight too many."

### MIRACLE

(PRECEDING PAGES) *Forty-six years and ten months old, George Foreman regains the World Championship. With a single blow he overpowered Michael Moorer. A true miracle! (November, 1994) Axel Schulz tried to resist Foreman but lost by decision. (April 1995)* (OPPOSITE) *Foreman is eternal.*

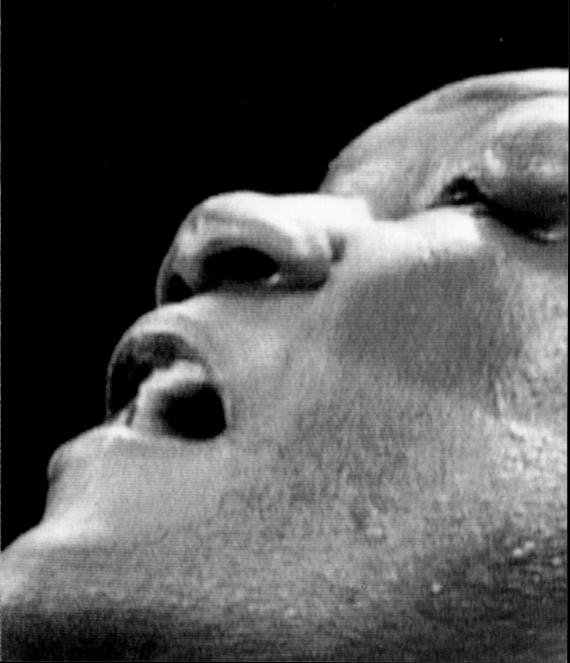

EVANDER

# holyfield

**A champion cut to measure**

**A REAL WORK HORSE**

*Thanks to a rigorous training regime, Evander Holyfield sculpted himself a body of steel.*
*He would need it when he moved up into the heavyweight division. (November 1995)*

**"Holyfield stepped into Tyson's shoes, but they were too big for him."**
If you want to irritate Evander Holyfield, that's all it takes. At the beginning of this decade, the boxer from Atlanta met up with James Buster Douglas, the unknown who had destroyed Tyson's myth. Holyfield won the fight, *and* the unified World Heavyweight Championship. Even so, in the eyes of many boxing fans, Holyfield was an overrated boxer. He certainly had big dreams when, as Cruiserweight Champion, he decided to move up a division. But these days, if you remind him of his past, he says it's the size of the heart that matters, not the size of the man.

In the end, it was the challenge that mattered more than anything. Besides, the prize money available these days makes up for the hardest "punch" a sarcastic journalist can throw. So Holyfield took up body-building. In only a few months, he put on about twenty-five pounds of muscle. His hard work paid off and after a few years he'd earned over a hundred and ten million dollars. After having watched this spectacular physical transformation, his detractors accused him of using steroids. Holyfield took the offensive,

# EVANDER HOLYFIELD

## UNITED STATES

BORN OCTOBER 19, 1962

37 FIGHTS

34 WINS
(25 BY KO)

3 LOSSES

WBA WORLD CRUISERWEIGHT
CHAMPION FROM 1986 TO 1987

WBA-IBF WORLD CRUISERWEIGHT
CHAMPION IN 1987

UNIFIED WORLD CRUISERWEIGHT
CHAMPION IN 1988

UNIFIED WORLD HEAVYWEIGHT
CHAMPION FROM 1990 TO 1992

WBA-IBF WORLD HEAVYWEIGHT
CHAMPION FROM 1993 TO 1994

WBA WORLD HEAVYWEIGHT
CHAMPION SINCE 1997

and replied, in a statement aimed at schoolchildren: "Don't believe that Evander takes steroids. I'm not a cheater. And I never was. I work hard, very hard, and it's paid off for me. Be like me. Don't take drugs. Be honest with yourselves, be fair, and work hard." As he defended himself, he was thinking about his own "Little E's," as he calls his six children: Evander Jr. (eleven), Evette (ten), Ebony (eight), Ewin (five), Emani (three), and Eden (a few months).

Holyfield is courageous—a warrior of the ring. Pride, will, professionalism—there aren't enough adjectives to describe his stance against an adversary. He likes to say that he was "born to win." Or, as the embroidery on one of his many satin jackets reads: "I am more than a conqueror." And it's true. But although he was surrounded by the pomp of a perfect champion, he hadn't yet challenged Mike Tyson.

The match that Holyfield was counting on to raise him to the ranks of stardom was scheduled for November 1991. But Tyson forfeited the match because of an injury. A few months later, Tyson landed in prison. Those who still questioned Holyfield's powers didn't hesitate to say he'd been saved by a miracle. The fighter defended himself, insisting that there's not a boxer in the world he was afraid of fighting. To prove it, he lined up three extraordinary fights against Riddick Bowe.

It was November 13, 1992. Holyfield was fighting for one reason: respect. He demanded recognition, especially after two difficult successes, on points, against George Foreman and Larry Holmes, the "granddaddies" of the division. He went on to beat James Buster Douglas in his only victory by knockout (KO in Round Four) in a World Championship fight. But boxing specialists still didn't think Holyfield had what it took to be a heavyweight. At thirty years old, Holyfield was a rich man. He'd pocketed close to fifteen million dollars, most notably against Foreman. But after twenty-two years spent in the ring, he was getting tired. He began to wonder if he wasn't slowly killing himself with stubborn hopes. And for what? Money was no problem, and he'd always insisted he wasn't fighting for the glory. But he couldn't resist the allure of one more challenge. One year later, on November 6, 1993, Holyfield fought a rematch against Bowe. He was out to regain his standing as number one, and to prove that he could still take on a big, young heavyweight. At Caesar's Palace in Las Vegas, the challenger took back his WBA and IBF belts, winning on points. Now the press had to respect him.

Holyfield compared becoming champion again to being born again. Six months later,

# "IF YOU'VE ALREADY WON ENOUGH MONEY, AND YOU AREN'T IN IT FOR THE GLORY, WHY GO ON?"

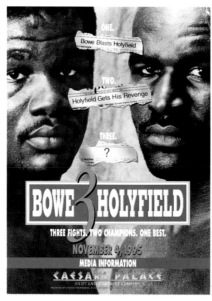

**QUITE A PROGRAM**

*On November 4, 1995, Evander Holyfield and Riddick Bowe
found themselves on the same poster for the third time.*

Holyfield spoke to a young audience, evoking his faith in God. On his T-shirt was written: "Property of God." The occasion was a final public training session before a match against ex-middleweight lefty Michael Moorer. But facing Moorer, Holyfield seemed to be all alone in the world. In a weakened state, he quickly lost both world titles, as well as his faith in the sport which had brought him so much. After the match, he was forced to undergo medical testing because of a mild illness. The results were shocking. Holyfield had a defective heart, a problem with his left ventricle. He was forbidden to fight for one year. But Holyfield insisted he was only dehydrated after the fight. Experts brought in for a second opinion confirmed that he was "fit to box." "Jesus saved me," he said, and went on to describe how, in June of 1994, he went to see a Baptist healer. When the healer put his hands on Holyfield's heart, the boxer said he was filled with warmth, and then fell, unconscious, to the ground. When he arose, he was healed. The healer then invited Holyfield to testify about his experience on television. After the lights went down and the cameras

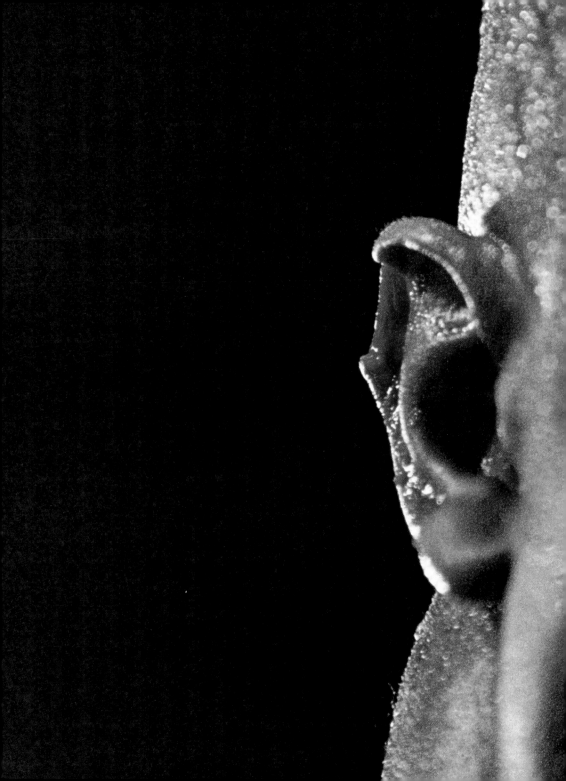

were turned off, the healer turned to Holyfield and told him that he had been chosen by God, and that he also had special healing powers. Men and women lined up in front of the fighter. And, Holyfield recounts that each time he touched them, they too were filled with warmth, and then fell down unconscious.

With God's help, Holyfield was convinced that he could be Heavyweight Champion for a third time. He said everyone else was afraid of fighting Bowe—but he had done so three times. Actually, since Holyfield refused the WBO title after Bowe let it go, there was no title at stake for this third Holyfield vs. Bowe match-up. Even so, the fight was supposed to prove which man was the best boxer in the division. Having earned enough belts and crowns, the man from Atlanta was fighting for glory now—and for money. The fight got off to a fast start. Holyfield was KO'd for the first time ever by Bowe, and it seemed that the "champion with a heart" had come to the end of his career. But then, on May 11, 1996, thirty-three-year-old Holyfield returned to Madison Square Garden. And once there, he showed that he was still a presence among heavyweights. In five passable rounds, he beat fellow American Bobby Czyz, an ex-Cruiserweight and Light Heavyweight Champion. There was still hope for a Tyson-Holyfield meeting.

The two men finally met late in 1996, at the MGM, Las Vegas. The stakes were twenty-five to one in favor of Tyson. But Holyfield's mental strength, physique, and sense of resolution allowed him to win over the Tyson fury. By the eleventh round, Holyfield was declared the strongest. He proved it again nearly eight months later in only three rounds—a bout that ended in Tyson's disqualification. In the battle, Holyfield lost part of his right ear and Tyson the little credibility which he still had. Holyfield came out the undisputed champion, both in the ring and in the hearts and minds of the boxing world.

**BOWE VS. HOLYFIELD**

*The two men had it out, blow by blow, during three fights and thirty-two rounds.
In the thirty-second round, Holyfield stayed on the canvas, KO'd (November 1995)*
**(PRECEDING PAGES)** *Holyfield's right ear in the third round of his fight against Tyson.
MGM Grand Garden Arena, Las Vegas June 28, 1997.*

# RIDDICK

# B

# bowe

## Champion of a new generation

## RIDDICK BOWE

### UNITED STATES

**BORN AUGUST 10, 1967**

**41 FIGHTS**

**40 WINS**
**(33 BY KO)**

**1 LOSS**

**UNIFIED WORLD HEAVYWEIGHT**
**CHAMPION IN 1992**

**WBA-IBF WORLD HEAVYWEIGHT**
**CHAMPION IN 1993**

**WBO WORLD HEAVYWEIGHT**
**CHAMPION SINCE 1995**

**AN INSEPARABLE DUO**

*With the help of his manager, Rock Newman, Riddick Bowe became
the "official" World Heavyweight Champion of the late nineties. (November 1995)*

**"When I'm World Champion and one of the most famous athletes on the planet,
I plan to use my name to make the world a better place for people of all colors.
I'll be an example. You can count on me."** On the boxing circuit, Bowe is known as
"Big Daddy." The name refers to the size of his family, not to his heavyweight physique.
The fighter and his wife, Judith, have seven children. It sounds like a lot, right? For Bowe,
it's normal—he comes from a family of thirteen kids, all raised by his mother, Dorothy.

As for Riddick's dream, it's still just that—a dream. Because among the heavyweights of
today, Tyson is king. Riddick is still far from attracting the media attention that his
"brother," also from Brooklyn, merits. And yet, ever since his third face-off with Evander
Holyfield, Bowe had been considered number one in the division. But the shadow of
Tyson is always there in the background. Until "Big Daddy" proves himself against his
nemesis, Bowe will remain at the top, but never number one.

Joe Frazier, Ken Norton, Larry Holmes, Michael Spinks—the list of illustrious pugilists to
have passed through trainer Eddie Futch's capable hands is impressive. And Futch, eighty-

three years old, couldn't stop singing his young trainee's praises. He compared Riddick's agility to Ali, his jab to that of Larry Holmes. Of course, Bowe didn't want to disappoint the man who told him he could be the best. Most of all, Bowe didn't want to disappoint himself as he had in the heavyweight match for the gold at the '88 Olympic games in Seoul. Beaten by Lennox Lewis, Bowe's reputation collapsed, in part because of the rumors spread by Ray Mercer, his roommate during the games, claiming Bowe talked constantly about being afraid of his adversary. Bowe became known as a loser. Only Rock Newman, his new manager, still saw millions of dollars in the young boxer's future. In a division where size is everything, his true heavyweight physique—six feet four and about 240 pounds—gives him the power to destroy his adversaries.

He gave it his all and got his first chance at a world title, on Friday 13, November 1992. His opponent was Evander Holyfield. Bowe was absolutely sure that Holyfield would finish the fight flat on his back. And he did knock Holyfield off his feet, for the first time in the older man's career. After an incredible round eleven, Holyfield finally went down. Bowe won on points in the "fight of 1992." A new star was in the skies, a star without any worries. Riddick had finally proven that besides being a fine puncher, he also had the all-important attributes of bravery and class. At twenty-five years old, with seven million dollars in prize money in his bank account, his adventures had just begun.

"When I'm champion...," Bowe used to say—and now he was. This was his chance to stand by his words. He embarked on a world tour, stopping to shake hands with Pope John Paul II; he met Nelson Mandela; offered his support to the ANC; visited Somalia; and continued to support President Clinton. Trainer Eddie Futch finally told Riddick to remember that boxing came first. The matches continued. Bowe successfully defended his title against "strawmen" Michael Dokes and Jesse Ferguson, pocketing seven million dollars in prize money per fight. But the day of his return match against Evander Holyfield rolled around all too soon. The big young boxer had fought only three rounds in one year. On November 6, 1993, he put his IBF and WBA titles on the line. And the WBC title? He threw it away in front of flashing cameras at a news conference. The gesture symbolized how Bowe and his trainer felt about Don King's ultimate control over the federation. It was, in short, a declaration of war.

**RESPECT**

*Bowe admits: "Holyfield has become a friend to me, but I still hate him in the ring"*

Against Holyfield, the fight was closer than the previous one. It was also full of surprises. A parachutist landed on the ropes of the ring, right in the middle of the match. The fight was interrupted for twenty minutes, which was a long time for both fighters to sit and stew. When the two men returned to the ring, Holyfield took command, and, in the end, regained his title, by decision. Bowe was champion no longer. And in a world where Don King wielded more and more power, Bowe was going to wait a long time for the chance to regain his dream. He grabbed the WBO title, making quick work of Englishman Herbie Hide and Cuban Jorge Gonzales. But his true test would have to wait. Mike Tyson was still in prison. Only Evander Holyfield had the power to make Bowe number one again. After twenty-four rounds, the two men were almost "friends." On November 4, 1995, they found themselves once again in opposing corners of a ring, for a rematch with no title at stake. But the fact remained—the winner of this fight would be considered the world's number one boxer. It was a cliff-hanger, and Bowe took it in the eighth round. Holyfield came close to winning in round five, but in the end he was KO'd. Then, in July, at Madison Square Garden, it was not just the boxers who found themselves knocked off their feet. The end of a match between Bowe and Andrew Golota, from Poland, turned into one of the worst brawls in the sport's history. When Golota was disqualified after too many low blows, the Bowe entourage decided to take his punishment into their own hands. The fans joined the fray, and the riot, fought along racial lines, quickly got out of hand.

On December 14, 1996, Bowe and Golota staged a highly awaited rematch. But in many ways it looked like a repeat. Bowe couldn't get the upper hand, and even went down in the second and fifth rounds. Golota, who was in difficulty in the fourth round and even went down himself, was ahead on points. But his many low blows cost him an almost certain victory. As in the first fight he was disqualified, this time in the ninth round. These two fights put Bowe through a lot, and he very much wanted to get a new start in life. He decided to join the Marines for three years, only to resign less than a week after signing up when he realized that the training was too tough. He quit boxing definitively at the end of April 1997 and began a new career on cable TV.

### A TRUE HEAVYWEIGHT

(OPPOSITE) *At six feet four and weighing two-hundred and forty pounds, Riddick Bowe has one of the most impressive heavyweight physiques on the planet.* (PRECEDING PAGES) *In the end, Bowe's power wins out over Holyfield's heart.*

BRUCE

# seldon

A champion from the "lower depths"

# LIKE TWO OF HIS ILLUSTRIOUS PREDECESSORS,

Boxing is sometimes about having "big fists." For Bruce Seldon—otherwise known as "The Atlantic City Express"—it's also a case of a big heart. Physically, Seldon is an example of a perfectly proportioned heavyweight. Psychologically, he is also an example. With the help of the Sweet Science, he'd made a complete break from a troubled adolescence. Even more impressive, he learned how to box—in prison. Arrested for armed robbery at the age

# SONNY LISTON AND MIKE TYSON, IT WAS WITHIN

of sixteen, he didn't receive his walking papers until four years later, in 1987. During those four years, he became Heavyweight Champion in the New Jersey interprison tournaments. He won twenty of the twenty-four matches he fought while behind bars. Even before his prison stay, Seldon had been passionate about boxing. His mother, Joan Graham, who worked in an Atlantic City casino, would give him free tickets to the fights. After leaving prison, Seldon went home to Atlantic City, a place where temptation is lurking behind every shop window and around every corner. Luckily for Bruce Seldon, the late '80s were a time of change and growth for Atlantic City. The city's promoters were out to dethrone Las Vegas as the gaming capital of America. Casinos were springing up every-

# THE FOUR WALLS OF A PENITENTIARY THAT SELDON

where, and it seemed like money was growing on trees. It worked out well for Seldon, who wanted to make amends for his past. He made a promise to his mother that he would never return to prison. In 1988, the little heavyweight—only six feet two inches tall—turned pro. He quickly began to accumulate victories. Busy enjoying his successes, Seldon neglected his training for the sake of partying.

On April 18, 1991, Holyfield was up against Foreman at the Atlantic City Convention Center. There were the usual opening fights, the perfect showcase for some of boxing's young hopefuls. One of these hopefuls was Seldon. Facing the "Atomic Taurus," Oliver McCall, he started out leading on points. But as the fight went on, his lack of conditioning became more and more apparent. Finally, in the ninth round, he was KO'd. Seldon

# FOUND A REASON TO LIVE . . .

**BRUCE SELDON**

UNITED STATES

BORN JANUARY 30, 1967

37 FIGHTS

33 WINS
(29 BY KO)

4 LOSSES

WBA WORLD HEAVY-
WEIGHT CHAMPION
FROM 1995 TO 1996

# ATLANTIC CITY

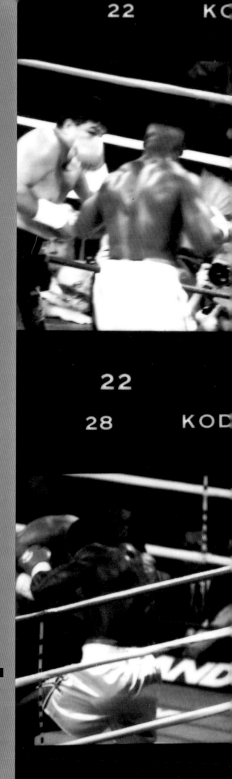

attributed the loss to overconfidence and being out-of-shape. He began to have doubts about dedicating himself entirely to the sport, but he realized that without boxing he'd still be on the streets. Four months later, he fought for the first time after his big loss. He faced a real challenge. Opposite him in the ring was the 1988 Olympic gold medal winner, Riddick Bowe. It was a risky choice for a boxer who had lost his last match by a KO. And Seldon would pay the price for his daring.

In front of a hometown crowd at Atlantic City, he was destroyed in the first round. It was not hard to figure out why. Seldon had the body of Hercules, but he couldn't roll with the punches. One year later, his difficulties were confirmed. He found himself on the canvas again, and lost in ten rounds on points to Tony "TNT" Tubbs, ex-World Champion. Seldon's career was on the rocks. But he had made a promise to his mother. For her sake, he kept at it, and proceeded to carry off seven victories by KO. Seldon signed on with Don King, who was keen for new heavyweight talent now that Tyson was behind bars.

With Tyson's imprisonment, anarchy took over in the boxing world. The chaos was a lucky break for Bruce Seldon. Between August 2, 1987, and November 13, 1992, the heavyweight title was unified. In every other division, the title was divided three ways. The WBC, the WBA, and the IBF each recognized a different middleweight champion, bantamweight champion, and welterweight champion. But with the heavies, it was different. Mike Tyson, James Buster Douglas, and Evander Holyfield were, each in his turn, the official "strongest man in the world." Then, in November 1992, Evander Holyfield was beaten by Riddick Bowe. Bowe and his manager, Rock Newman, had taken it upon themselves to fight a two-man battle against the growing power of boxing promoters. In front of the flashing cameras of a news conference, Bowe threw his WBC belt into a garbage can. The title was effectively divided into two. The WBA and the IBF recognized Bowe as World Champion, while the WBC rolled out the red carpet for Englishman Lennox Lewis. As 1995 got underway, the situation worsened. The WBA and the IBF took George Foreman's title away from him. Now two titles stood vacant. The WBA decided to pit Seldon against Tony "TNT" Tucker. Tucker, a real hard-hitting tiger, was nonetheless no longer the boxer he once was. He was thirty-five-years-old, and showing the signs of a long and hard fight against drugs. Seldon was ultra-conscious of the doubt in everyone's minds. He moved constantly throughout the fight, and finally landed a direct punch to Tony Tucker's eye, injuring the older boxer. The match continued. Seldon dominated, thanks to his vitality and fighting intelligence. Tucker's eye swelled up like a golf ball and his nose was twice its normal size. Finally, the referee consulted with the ring doctor and stopped the fight. Tucker was furious. Seldon became world champion in a fight stopped because of injury. The man who was born in Atlantic City, and saw his two greatest failures there, triumphed in Las Vegas. But he wanted to return to his hometown to defend his title. Impossible. New Jersey's boxing commission had forbidden Don King, Seldon's promoter, to organize fights anywhere in the state. Soon Seldon had other business on his mind—like coming to terms with the recent death of his mother. He placed his championship belt on her grave. The "Atlantic City Express" had kept his promise. Bruce Seldon began to donate much of his time to organizations that fight teen-age drug abuse and delinquency.

August 19, 1995, was the date of Tyson's return. Seldon defended his title in an opening match against the first Native American to have a chance at the heavyweight title—Joe Hipp. Without style or panache, but with the help of his 230 pounds of muscle and a newly strengthened will to win, Seldon dominated once again. He caught Hipp with an explosive jab, and the fight was stopped in the eighth round.

Seldon was world champion. But what could he do against Mike Tyson? Seldon never stopped saying that to beat Tyson you need three things: "style, conditioning, and will power." But, on September 7, 1996, the man from Atlantic City didn't have any of these, least of all the determination he so desperately needed. Smiling as he climbed into the ring, he left one minute and forty-nine seconds later after a mockery of a fight. Seldon, terrified by how much was at stake, barely threw a punch. The man who had dreamed of going home to New Jersey as the man who beat Tyson didn't live up to his championship belt. The life of Bruce Seldon illustrates how the world of boxing is a place where a man can win it all by moving from the four walls of a cell to the four ropes of a ring. The "Atlantic City Express" chose his own nickname as a symbol of his amazing ascension, and his rapid victories. But like a train moving from station to station, a career in boxing slows down after a while. A fighter just runs out of steam. For Bruce Seldon, however, what matters is that he kept his promise, and that he changed his lifestyle along the way. Now he knows what it's like to travel First Class.

LARRY

# holmes

Champion of missed chances

**Along with George Foreman, this man is one of the "granddaddies" of boxing.**
Like Foreman, he left the ring, only to return again, unable to resist the idea of finally being recognized for his true worth. Of course, he also had his eyes on the prizes his younger counterparts were cashing in on. Unlike "Big George," Ali, and Tyson, Larry Holmes' reputation as a big league boxer is not indisputable. The life of a boxing star often rests on a scanty foundation. The smallest mistake, the least suspicion about your capabilities, and your reputation is tarnished for years to come.

Larry Holmes entered amateur boxing in 1968. He fought in the tryouts for the '72 American Olympic team, knowing that a medal would be his entrée into the boxing business as well as the key to financial reward. But disillusionment soon set upon Holmes. During a qualifying round, he was knocked off his feet. Panicking, he crawled out of the ring on his hands and knees! Courage—without which talent, power, work, and charisma are nothing—had abandoned the young boxer at the worst possible time.

Suddenly he was trying to build a professional career on the foundations of a terrible reputation. In an arena where mistakes aren't easily forgiven, no one could forget Holmes' descent into the depths of fear. On March 21, 1973, for his first professional fight, he earned only sixty-three dollars, while the lucky Olympic medal winners were pocketing tens of millions of dollars for their matches. Finally, Don King overlooked the young boxer's difficult past and hired him as a sparring partner for his "stable of fighters," which included the great Ali. Although King wasn't particularly thrilled by Holmes at first, the boxer's left jab became more and more dangerous. The promoter began to notice this "dark horse" among his fighters. And on June 9, 1978, at the ripe old age of twenty-nine, Holmes' dream came true. The occasion was a now legendary fight against Ken Norton. This time, despite an arm injury, Holmes didn't run away. The fifteenth round was extraordinary, but Holmes left the ring triumphant, the winner by decision. He was finally World Heavyweight Champion, but at the worst possible moment in boxing history.

Six months earlier, he would have been crowned unified champion, like his predecessors Ali, Frazier, and Foreman. But the war of the promoters had begun to rage, and the federations were "troubling and doubling boxing's hierarchy." Holmes was only the WBC champion. Charismatic Ali still held the WBA belt. In other words, Holmes wasn't a "direct descendant" in the line of champions: the champion who beat the champion who had beaten the champion before him.

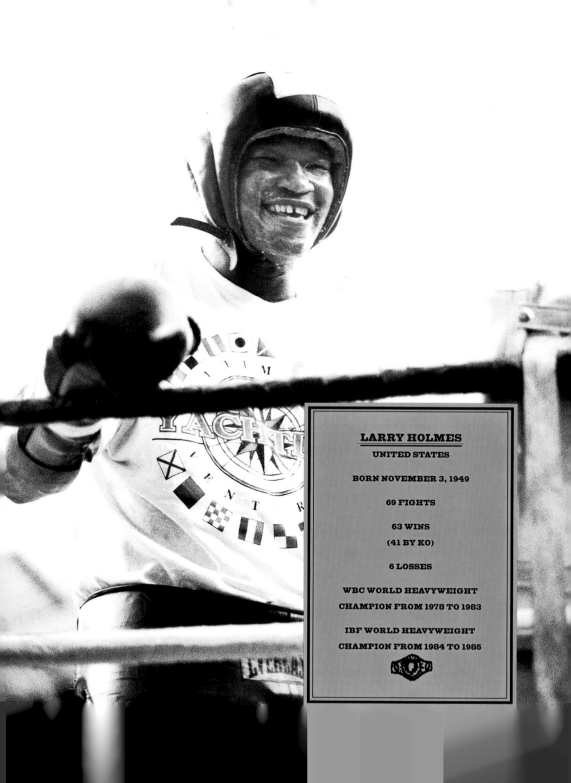

**LARRY HOLMES**

UNITED STATES

BORN NOVEMBER 3, 1949

69 FIGHTS

63 WINS
(41 BY KO)

6 LOSSES

WBC WORLD HEAVYWEIGHT
CHAMPION FROM 1978 TO 1983

IBF WORLD HEAVYWEIGHT
CHAMPION FROM 1984 TO 1985

Over the next two years, he defended his title seven times, and won every time with a KO. Boxing fans started calling him "The Assassin from Easton," his Pennsylvania hometown. But the American public was still skeptical. Old stories die hard, and no matter how hard Holmes could hit, he still couldn't overcome the doubts.

On October 2, 1980, Holmes believed he was about to fight the match that would finally give him a place among the greats. Everyone else remained skeptical. And in the end, the evening with the strange title—"Last Applause"—turned out to be a nightmare for Holmes. Ali, whom he had so often faced as a sparring partner, was already showing signs of the illness that would incapacitate him just a few years later. An avalanche of jabs hammered the old champion. **"The butterfly" or "the bee," as he used to be called, was just another thirty-eight-year-old boxer, whose wings had been clipped for some time now.** As the bell was rung for the eleventh round, the referees refused to allow Ali to continue, holding him in his corner. The Caesar's Palace crowd was relieved. Despite his win, the evening hadn't been a success for Holmes. He hadn't gained a thing in terms of public opinion, and he went down in history as the man who put an end to the career of one of the greatest boxers ever, an idol for the last twenty years.

Holmes would go on to defend his title twenty times, but would never succeed in becoming Unified Champion. After breaking with Don King, he won the IBF crown, recently created in 1984, and became "one-third" of a champion. While this was nothing to write home about, the boxer was simply a victim of his times.

And yet, with a perfect record after his last forty-eight fights, the man who'd won twenty-one consecutive championship bouts could hope to tie the record held by another Heavyweight World Champion, Rocky Marciano. Marciano could claim victory forty-nine times out of forty-nine fights. **At thirty-five years of age, Holmes hoped to finally enter the hall of fame. On September 22, 1985, he took on Michael Spinks, an ex-Middleweight Champion. But once again he stumbled and lost by decision. So close to the crown he almost touched it, he'd lost his last chance for glory.** "The Assassin from Easton" was "assassinated" at the worst possible time. He would never manage to return to his old form. One year later, he lost badly in his rematch against Michael Spinks, and this time he decided to retire and return to Easton. By leaving the scene, he helped Mike Tyson in his rise to power. Tyson finally did what Holmes never could—he became the only Heavyweight Champion in the world by reuniting the three titles.

Then Holmes decided to risk everything and try for a comeback. In 1988, he challenged Tyson, saying he knew how perilous boxing could be, but there were risks everywhere, and he planned to keep fighting until someone made him stop. And that's not all. He called Tyson a "son of a bitch," and said he was destined to end up behind bars. That was a big mistake. In the fourth round, Tyson made him pay for his rash words. Holmes was knocked out, for the first and only time in his career. Three years later, the drama began again. Holmes laced up his gloves one more time, and ignored the snide remarks about his age circulating in the press. In fact, he came up with a few remarks of his own, saying that the journalists weren't exactly spring chickens either. Used to receiving regular retirement checks from all his earnings in the ring, **Holmes was a victim of the "Foreman syndrome." He was jealous of the other boxers' fame and fortune.**

In 1991, he faced fellow American Ray Mercer, the 1988 Olympic champion. Finally, Holmes had the chance to rid himself of bad memories. Helped by his years of experience, he outfoxed Mercer with the surprising force of his jab and won the fight, no contest. This time, the path was clear to a championship match against Evander Holyfield. At stake was a seven million dollar purse, and, most importantly, the chance to finally become Unified World Heavyweight Champion. But once again, at a pivotal moment in his career, Holmes choked. He lost the match by decision and left the fight with a detached retina, requiring surgery. This would be the end of his career.

Almost. When he was nearly forty-six years old, he met WBC champion Oliver McCall for one more fight. The two men were fighting for the modest sum of three hundred and fifty thousand dollars. This time Holmes had finally had enough. He announced that if he lost this match he would retire once and for all. And he did lose, after twelve mediocre rounds.

Finally sure of what he wanted, Holmes returned home to Easton to be with his children and grandchildren. Well known and respected, he looked forward to a peaceful retirement—or did he? In June of 1996 he was back in the ring—and again in 1997. He said he'd talked it over with his wife, Diane, and she told him to do whatever he thought best— but *do it!*

### GRANDDADDY HOLMES

*Throughout his long career, Larry Holmes remained good-humored.*
*He deserves a place in the history books.*

# LENNOX

# L

# lewis

The quest of a champion

**AMBITIOUS**

**(ABOVE)** *Since his success at the 1988 Olympics in Seoul, Lewis has had one goal:
total domination of the heavyweight division.*
**(FOLLOWING PAGES)** *Lewis, beaten and humiliated against McCall. (September 1994)*

" **LEWIS IS BORN TO BE BRITISH. HIS NAME PROVES IT. : L FOR LONDON, E FOR ENGLAND, W FOR WALES, I FOR IRELAND AND S FOR SCOTLAND ."**

The play on words came from Lennox's manager, Frank Maloney. It was right on target. And yet, London-born Lewis left the city at the age of twelve to live with his mother in Canada. As a result, when he won the heavyweight gold at the '88 Olympics in Seoul, the anthem he heard while standing on the podium was Canadian. Treason? No, because in 1994 he was Heavyweight World Champion again, this time under the English flag.

And so it goes in boxing's history. Countries vie for champions, and playing dirty is always allowed in a world where, by definition, any blow is within limits. Often it's a champion's entourage who are really the masters of the game. Lewis said he wanted to make a name for himself, before confronting Donovan Ruddock on October 31, 1992, in London. Ruddock was a true Canadian, and the match, a true WBC World Championship semi-final. The fight's name said it all: "The Fight for the Right." The victor won the right to confront the title-holding champion. In other words, it was the first step towards the stardom for which Lewis longed. He knew Ruddock all too well because they'd fought in many training rounds back home in Canada, and Lewis had already beaten him in amateur fights. This time, he was ready to start winning all over again. And he did. After only two rounds, thanks to a thunderous right, Lewis destroyed his ex-training partner, ex-compatriot, ex-adversary. Ruddock was no longer a contender in the race to fame.

Lewis, on the other hand, had just taken a giant step towards glory. Without knowing it, he'd become a potential world champion. Because a few months later, Riddick Bowe had it out with the WBC and gave up his belt. Lewis was rewarded for Bowe's defection—with the WBC Heavyweight World Championship. If only it could always be so easy. "I'm the first subject of Her Majesty the Queen to win the heavyweight title, but I know that if I'd lost the match, I'd just be another good-for-nothing Canadian." The achievement was unprecedented since 1899. Of course, in reality, Lewis only possessed a fourth of a title.

If you want to make it big as a heavyweight, crossing the Atlantic is obligatory. The road to worldwide recognition runs through Las Vegas. Lewis claims he's got "American style" *and* British boxing skills. He showed up in the U.S. to confront Tony Tucker and set off to "win over the Americans." Since the turn of the century, fourteen British contenders to the heavyweight throne had been beaten by their U.S. rivals. The challenge was immense. But Lewis was sure of himself. He had reason to be. At thirty-four, Tony Tucker's best years were behind him. Tucker went down in the third round, but managed to get up again. The same thing happened again in the ninth. In the end, Lewis beat him by decision. But the victory wasn't particularly decisive, and the American public wasn't sure what to make of this brash young Englishman. Lewis just wasn't convincing. He had excuses—like a bad tendon injury in the little finger of his right hand, which eventually landed him in the hospital for an operation. Still, a spoke had been put in the wheel of his American campaign.

**LENNOX LEWIS**

GREAT BRITAIN

BORN SEPTEMBER 2, 1965

31 FIGHTS

30 WINS

(25 BY KO)

1 LOSS

WBC WORLD HEAVYWEIGHT

CHAMPION IN 1994 and 1997

ATLANTIC CITY. MAY 6, 1994.

# "YOU'LL SEE HOW MUCH PROGRESS I'VE MADE!"

THE AMERICAN PRESS REMAINS

# SKEPTICAL

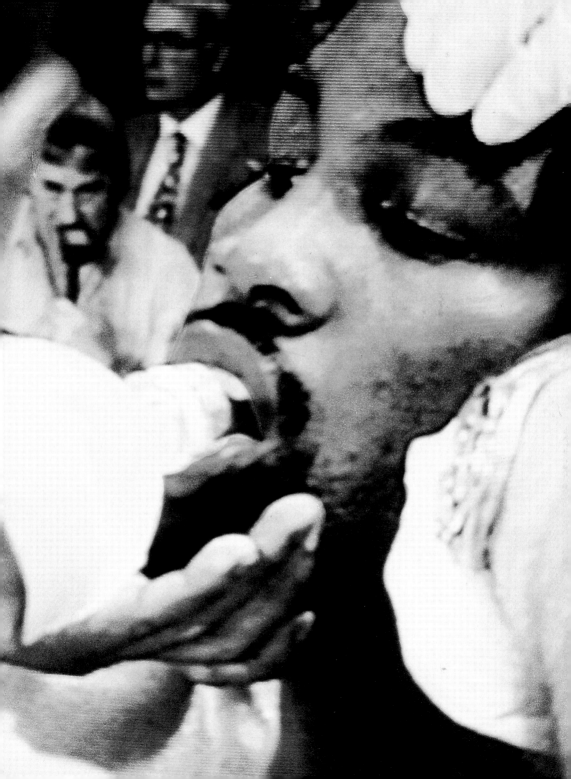

Back to England. Lewis decided to take on the ultra-popular Frank Bruno, "the loser that England loves." This was the man who was a regular at Buckingham Palace, and who was designated as a Member of the British Empire (MBE). He'd known glory, but he'd also known tears. Written on his visiting card was the story of two big losses, against Tim Witherspoon and Mike Tyson. October 1, 1993, wasn't going to be the day of Bruno's redemption. He bowed before the power of Lewis' punches. The referee stopped the fight in the seventh round. This was a hard blow, because until then, Bruno had been leading on points. Before the fight, Lewis had sworn to leave his homeland if he lost. But even though he won, he hadn't convinced anyone of his powers, so he took off again to conquer America. He headed towards Atlantic City. On May 6, 1994, he confronted an unknown, Phil Jackson. Lewis hardly had to touch Jackson—three punches and his adversary went down three times. The referee stopped the blood-bath in the eighth round. But the American press was still skeptical. Sportswriters accused the Brit of being a flash-in-the-pan. They said he didn't have the killer instinct. It became clear that Lewis' only fault was not being American. The editors of *The Sun* and *The Daily Mirror* had no doubts whatsoever. As far as they were concerned, Lewis was on his way towards gaining the unified title, and keeping it—all the way into the twenty-first century.

That day was still far in the future. But the first obstacle, on September 24, 1994, shouldn't have been insurmountable. For his first fight in London with a title at stake, Lewis met up with Oliver McCall, one of Don King's protégés. As usual, Lewis had things to say about his adversary: he said he'd worked too hard to lose his title in a little fight. He called McCall a loser. Then he predicted that if McCall made the mistake of leaving his chin open, he would be KO'd for the first time in his career. The prediction proved to be true—except for one small detail. It was Lewis who got blasted on the chin.

In only two rounds, his dreams of grandeur were destroyed. The first loss of his career shook Lewis to the core. The month of his twenty-ninth birthday was a time of soul-

## AIM: TO RECONQUER THE TITLE

(OPPOSITE) *After loosing his world title, Lewis found the road to success once again when he faced Tommy Morrison. (October 1995)*
(PRECEDING PAGES) *In the boxing world, the road to glory always passes through the United States.*
*Following tradition, Lewis went to Atlantic City to defend his title against Jackson.*
*But who you fight against is as important as whether you win or lose.*
*Jackson wasn't a true test of Lennox's powers. (May 1994)*

searching for the English boxer. Lewis wasn't getting any younger, and he couldn't find the right opponent. He had to wait for a whole year. Finally, he left again for the U.S., this time to meet up with the ex-"white hope" Tommy Morrison, who was also at a low point in his career and hoping for a new chance. The consequences of this match were far-reaching for both men, who fought each other with everything they had. Lewis seized his chance on October 7, 1995. Morrison went down four times before the match was stopped in the sixth. A few months later, Morrison encountered something more serious than anything inside the four ropes of a ring could ever be. A routine testing yielded shocking results: Morrison was HIV positive. He threw in his gloves and embarked on another kind of fight.

At over thirty years of age, Lewis was still a "new" boxer, still hoping to challenge Bowe, Tyson, and other world title holders. He wondered how he would ever become a champion without getting into championship fights. Tyson was the Englishman's true target. Lewis put himself in the hands of American justice, and was named obligatory challenger for the WBC title, which was then held by the American. Lewis cracked a bit under the pressure in New York's Madison Square Garden on May 11, 1996. Facing American Ray Mercer, ex-Olympic and WBO Heavyweight Champion, Lewis fought a difficult match. He won by decision. But the skeptics were still full of doubt.

Lewis had a rematch against Oliver McCall for the vacant WBC Heavyweight title in February 1997. The Las Vegas Hilton, which was back in the world of boxing, saw some of the most pitiful moments in the history of the Manly Art. McCall suffered a psychological breakdown and refused to fight. He took blow after blow without defending himself, but never went down. After five rounds of this non-fight, the ref stopped He wasn't all there, he was completely crazy", said Lewis after an evening when he regained the championship against the man who had humiliated him only two years earlier.

The victory was a sham, however. Lewis had seemed stronger that evening, but could he really beat Tyson or Holyfield? Even more, did he have what it takes to be a real champion?

**HONORS**

*Lewis receives the European Golden Glove award in Paris.*
*He was named best European boxer of the year*
*just before he lost his title.*

# M
## OLIVER
# mccall

From Tyson's sparring partner to champion—in one blow!

LENNOX LEWIS
WORLD CHAMPION
25 FIGHTS  25 WINS

OLIVER McCALL
DON KING'S CHALLENGER
29 FIGHTS  24 WINS

**HOUR OF GLORY**

**(ABOVE)** *McCall's finest hour, in London
as Lewis' vanquisher (September 1994)*
**(OPPOSITE)** *The hour has arrived. McCall's first title defense,
at Caesar's Palace, Las Vegas.*

It was September 24, 1994. No one in London believed that Oliver McCall had a chance against Lennox Lewis. Little did they know. After all, the boxer had already achieved one huge victory. He survived Chicago's infamous South Side and managed to escape. He lived the life of a typical adolescent there—violence, delinquency, a no-hope future. When this man swears it's kill or be killed, when he says, "This fight is the fight of my life," he isn't lying. McCall was going to make it, no matter what the cost. He asked the world not to judge him by his record, saying he accepted most of his fights on the run. Just ten days before a fight, he would start to train furiously.

The Englishman Lewis was taking this WBC World Heavyweight Championship lightly. He said McCall was a loser, would always be one. And it was true if you looked at the American's numbers. McCall had spent years taking blows as a sparring partner. But he hadn't been sparring against just anybody. During nearly three hundred training rounds,

OLIVER McCALL

UNITED STATES

BORN APRIL 21, 1965

33 FIGHTS
(18 BY KO)

26 WINS

7 LOSSES

WBC WORLD HEAVYWEIGHT
CHAMPION FROM 1994 TO 1995

"Don't judge me by my career record. I accepted most of my fights on the run, less than ten days before the scheduled date."

he had been weathering the storm of blows thrown at him by none other than the decade's most famous heavyweight, Mike Tyson. Not once during these rounds had he gone down. In fact, it was Tyson who had hit the ground during one of their sessions, for the first time in *his* career. McCall said that the difference between Tyson and Lewis was that Tyson had always respected him. And it was for Tyson, stagnating in prison for almost two-and-a-half years now, that McCall wanted to win this match. During the second round, a thunderous right hook sent Lewis reeling, a satisfactory reply to his over-confidence. The Englishman was in trouble, drowning in a London-like fog of blows. KO'd, he remained standing, held up by the arms of Mexican referee Mr. José Guadalupe Garcia. Garcia decided to stop the match in order to avoid a tragedy. "Kill or be killed." In one night, at Wembley Arena in the northern suburbs of London, McCall had destroyed Lewis' dreams of grandeur, and created the first glimmers of hope Tyson had seen in a long time. Suddenly, the whole world was listening to the voice bellowing through the compound:

# "And the new Heavyweight Champion of the World, Oliver MccccccCAAAAAALLLLL!"

The sparring partner-turned-champion offered his newly won title to the "master": "We got back your belt, Mike." Tyson was thrilled. Six months later, he was free. The whole world was waiting for him on April 8, 1995, at Caesar's Palace. He sat himself down in the front row, ready to contemplate this new champion: McCall. As for McCall, he was there to defend his title for the first time, against Larry Holmes. McCall was sure of one thing —Tyson didn't see him as just a sparring partner anymore.

McCall vs. Holmes. It was a surprising match-up since both men could boast of having been the sparring partner of a legendary boxer—the great Ali for Holmes, and Tyson for McCall. That evening, McCall justified his nickname: "Atomic Bull". His father had dubbed him so because in his early matches McCall had tended to charge his adversaries head on. He still came into the ring with the posture of a bull entering a stadium. This fight was no exception. The aging Holmes and his left jab teased McCall the way a toreador would tease a bull.

## HOLMES VS. MCCALL

*A boxer always needs to be surrounded by his own. McCall poses here with his mother. (April 1995)*
**(FOLLOWING PAGES)** *Facing Larry Holmes, McCall's youth destroys "The Assassin from Easton's" last chances for a world title. (April 1995)*

McCall started to stamp his feet. He couldn't get Tyson out of his mind. In 1988, Holmes had been knocked out by Tyson, who had been devastatingly strong in part because of all his work with Oliver McCall. The times had changed, and the passing seasons had slowed Holmes down. Even so, the Atomic Bull couldn't pierce the older fighter's guard. Holmes was, after all, forty-five years old. He'd been fighting professionally for twenty-two of those years. The fact that Holmes had a twenty-seven-year-old daughter, Misty, inevitably made one realize that he could have been McCall's father. The younger man managed to carry the fight, but only after a marathon that went to the limit. Victory, but unimpressive all the same.

It was September 2, 1995. McCall was still champion. He climbed into the ring at Wembley Arena knowing that twenty-seven members of his "clan," including his six children, had come all the way from America to give him their support. He needed them all, especially with an audience of forty thousand fans cheering the loser that England adored: Frank Bruno. This was Bruno's fourth chance at a world title, and he knew that it was now or never. He'd created the body of a gladiator—sculptured, impressive. Meanwhile, McCall had also been busy shopping. He had bought himself airplanes, as if he wanted to take off. As if he knew that he was in for a terrible crash-landing. For almost forty-five minutes, McCall refused to leave his dressing room. Finally, he entered the ring. Surprisingly, he seemed to be powerless. Before the fight, he had boasted of being able to punch eighty-five to one hundred times per round. In fact, he was roundly beaten, and barely escaped a KO. But he wouldn't fall down. He's only hit the ground one time in his life—when he was eighteen months old, and fell from a third story window. After the fall, he seemed more dead than alive.

Years later, the Atomic Bull was still standing, but he was destroying himself. Fighting another Brit, Lennox Lewis, whom he had beaten for the WBC heavyweight title in September 1994, McCall completely fell apart and refused to fight or even to defend himself. Battered by blows, he seemed to be in another world. Mills Lane, the referee, had to stop the fight. McCall had just come out of a detox center, after having failed to get off of alcohol and drugs. Two months later he was placed in a psychiatric hospital, and this time the injuries were obvious to all.

### MAN IN THE SHADOWS

*Behind a champion, there's always a man waiting in his corner. Chuck Bodak, eighty years old, is an important character in this story—the "champion of corner-men." (May 1995)*

# mccallum

## Champion of the shadows

In Kingston, Jamaica, "The Body Snatcher" is a national hero. The government has even issued a postage stamp in his honor. And yet, "Mike McCallum is one of the most underestimated athletes in boxing today. He's ageless." Bert Sugar, one of the great American boxing specialists, encapsulated the destiny of this boxer who, despite becoming the first world champion from Jamaica, in 1984, has never made it beyond glory to true stardom. McCallum spent the eighties in the shadow of the other great gloves of his time, men like Hagler, Hearns, and Leonard. Fed up with a lack of recognition from the American press, he finally announced that he was only fighting for one reason—the money. Which is why, like so many before him, McCallum refused to take a well-earned retirement. It was understandable. With style, mobility, a good eye, and years of experience in big fights, McCallum had perfected the science of avoiding punches. His energy and power would have been remarkable in a much younger man. Because of his elegance, both in and out of the ring, his admirers nicknamed him "the Professor." And it's true, McCallum has yet to come out of his corner with anything in mind except for putting on a show. He's there to do his job, to be a professional boxer. And to do it right.

He's done it right in championship matches against worthy opponents, men like Julian Jackson, KO in two rounds, in 1986; Donald Curry, taken down by a thundering hook in the fifth round in 1987; Michael Watson, staggering under McCallum's blows during a terrifying eleventh round in 1990; and Sumbu Kalambay, beaten in 1991 by decision, after what was perhaps McCallum's best ever demonstration of "his favorite tune." Sweet revenge for McCallum, who was set on winning decisively in order to forget his first loss, three years earlier, also on points. His second loss took place in 1992, when he took on another great fighter, James Toney, the speedy Middleweight Champion of that era, who clearly dominated the nearly thirty-six-year-old McCallum. By all rights, McCallum should already have been retired by then. But he didn't want to leave with the taste of defeat in his mouth. He knew that with his name alone a good promoter could create an event of worldwide proportions. So he came back for more, on the hunt for a new world title in 1994—the WBC Light Heavyweight crown, held at the time by Jeff Harding.

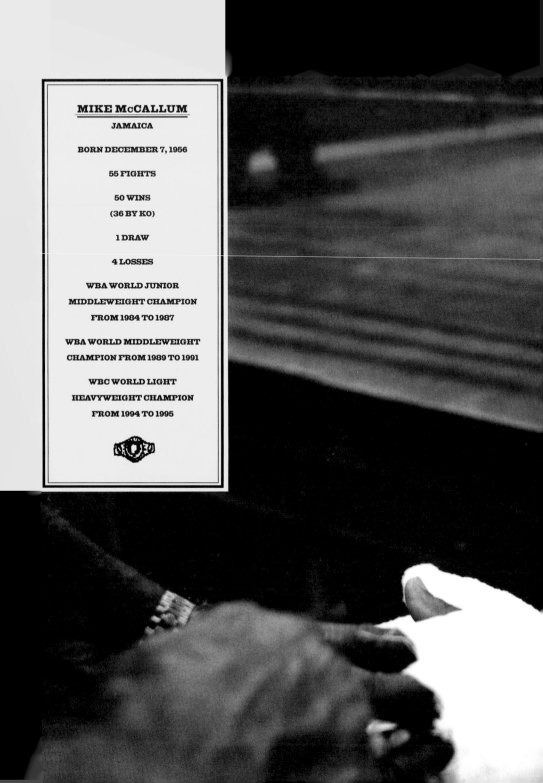

## MIKE McCALLUM

JAMAICA

BORN DECEMBER 7, 1956

55 FIGHTS

50 WINS
(36 BY KO)

1 DRAW

4 LOSSES

WBA WORLD JUNIOR
MIDDLEWEIGHT CHAMPION
FROM 1984 TO 1987

WBA WORLD MIDDLEWEIGHT
CHAMPION FROM 1989 TO 1991

WBC WORLD LIGHT
HEAVYWEIGHT CHAMPION
FROM 1994 TO 1995

He'd already been the proud bearer of the WBA Junior Middleweight and Middleweight crowns. Now, with the help of his experience, he'd won a third title in a third division. McCallum was ready to start all over again and told himself that it was a good thing he'd gained a few pounds. It's hard to imagine that as a child he wanted to be a jockey.

Glowing with the success of his new crown, he left for France, to defend his title on June 16, 1995, against Fabrice Tiozzo in Lyon. He arrived alone, without the man who had been his companion for years, eighty-three-year-old Eddie Futch, the "General of the ring." The two men made up a team where wisdom wasn't in short supply. McCallum said that Futch knew just what a boxer's limits were, especially McCallum's own. Eddie was always there to give his friend the advice he needed to win. But on that day, Futch was back home in Las Vegas, looking after his other trainee, Riddick Bowe. Without his corner-man, McCallum was lost. It was not the first time he'd had to look out for himself, but maybe it was one time too many. He was up against the best that boxing in France had to offer, and he was hit hard by Futch's absence, despite the presence of his second, Hedgemon Lewis.

The fight had barely started before the Jamaican found himself unable to keep up with the rhythm, the youth, the will, and the class of Tiozzo. Worse yet, for the first time in his career, one of McCallum's knees touched the ground in round two. It was the beginning of the end for a great champion, one who had never even graced the cover of a magazine. This third defeat, by decision, like the two preceding it, ought to have been a sign to McCallum that maybe it was time to throw in the towel. But that's not Mike's style. One and a half years later, he got a new chance for the world title, this time against Roy Jones. It was the old master against the young student. Experience against youth. McCallum was only able to last twelve rounds, but showed that he still had a place in the ring.

But after eighteen championship bouts, from 1984 to 1996, the years were finally taking their toll. Even so, at forty he still didn't want to turn in his gloves. "I feel like I'm twenty-five, with an added fifteen years experience." This is typical McCallum—slickly sidestepping a problem. He struggled to forget the death of his wife during an operation a few years earlier, saying, "You know I'll always be married to boxing." McCallum wants back in the ring, still pursuing his first true love.

# HAMPIONNAT DU MON

## "LE CHOC"

### MI-LOURDS - WBC - 12X3

**ABRICE**

**MIKE**

**IOZZO**

**CALLU**

## PALAIS DES SPORTS - LYON GERLAND

## VENDREDI 16 JUIN 1995 - 19H30

# tiozzo

The Tiozzo clan: family of champions

To head back to their roots is to head back towards the grim Paris suburb named St. Denis. It was there that Christophe and Fabrice Tiozzo grew up, along with older brother Frank. With Frank as a guide, Christophe and Fabrice dreamed of becoming world champions. And the dream came true, times two. The Tiozzo family is truly a family of champions.

Big brother Frank shared a passion for the ring with his two younger siblings. A professional boxer from 1979 until 1989, he never made it to the highest ranks. But that hardly matters now. Thanks to Christophe and Fabrice, he would be doubly compensated for his own difficulties. "When you're as gifted as Christophe, of course you make it. When you work as hard as Fabrice, of course you make it." Frank manages the careers of his kid brothers now, and watches them with a gaze that's both objective and admiring.

In 1984 Christophe took his place in the world of international boxing, winning a bronze medal at the Olympic games in Los Angeles. One year later, after his first pro season, he was France's Middleweight Champion. The seeds of a great champion were apparent in this young man, whom journalists began to compare to Marcel Cerdan. Ever since Cerdan's tragic early death and Jean-Claude Bouttier's success in the 1970s, France had been desperately searching for someone with enough star quality to rouse the public's interest in boxing again.

Christophe was the one. He won match after match, title after title. First came the European Middleweight Championship in 1988, then the WBA World Middleweight Championship on March 30, 1990. The fight, against Korean In-Chul Baek, was stopped in the sixth round. The three brothers came together at Lyon's boxing ring to celebrate the first world championship in the family. Fabrice, the "little fatso," as his brothers call him in allusion to his mania for dieting, was already a "vicarious" champion. But that was not enough. It only whetted his appetite.

Fabrice headed for Lyon, the "city of success," where he worked long and hard with his trainer and friend Jean Marc Perono. He spent any free time at the side of Michffile, the woman for whom he left his family when he was just sixteen years old. The real world started early for Fabrice, who immediately took on the responsibility of caring for and educating Bruno, Michffile's four-year-old son. This is a man who knows what he wants.

Meanwhile, Christophe was making the front pages of France's sporting journals. He defended his title against Paul Whitaker and Danny Morgan in 1990. Neither fight posed much danger. Against Panamanian Victor Cordoba in Marseilles on April 5, 1991,

**CHRISTOPHE TIOZZO**

FRANCE

BORN JUNE 1, 1963

35 FIGHTS

33 WINS
(22 BY KO)

2 LOSSES

WBA WORLD SUPER
MIDDLEWEIGHT CHAMPION
FROM 1990 TO 1991

he had something more to worry about. Fabrice, who entered the ring brandishing the WBA belt before the fight, had no idea what a setback his brother was about to face. In the ninth round, the referee rang the bell and stopped the match. Fabrice watched as the belt was pulled right out from under him. It was enough to bring tears to the eyes. Two months later, Fabrice was back in Lyon for the first big test of *his* professional career, a match-up with Eric Nicoletta. After his sixteenth victorious fight, he walked away from the ring brandishing another belt: the one that comes with the French Middleweight Championship. And now it belonged to him. While Frank was carefully laying the foundations of Fabrice's career, Christophe, managed by Jean-Christophe Courrffiges, was watching his own career crumble. After his first loss and a long vacation that was almost an early retirement, Christophe challenged Jeff Harding, the WBC World Middleweight Champion, on June 5, 1992. Again the match took place in Marseilles, and again the results were devastating. The only thing different about this fight was that the referee stopped it in the eighth round rather than the ninth. Christophe said farewell to the sport he loved so much.

Now it was all up to Fabrice. His first big chance was on April 3, 1993, against Virgil Hill, at Levallois. It was a case of youth against experience. Christophe was back in France after a long sojourn in the U.S., his preferred training grounds. With ringside seats, he couldn't keep still. He yelled at Fabrice to get back up again after two knockdowns at the beginning of the fight. Twenty-three-year-old Fabrice was affected, but not out of the fight. He hung on and came back again and again in a championship that he finally lost by decision. Not a morale booster. "Since that day," he said, "I've watched that fight hundreds of times, saying to myself, 'Never again.'" What he didn't say was that each time he turns the VCR off after his two falls. There's only so much one man can take. Marseilles or Levallois, the place hardly mattered when the results were the same. Only Lyon seemed to bring good luck to the Tiozzo brothers. One year later, Fabrice returned to his favorite town, ready to make a name for himself. His opponent, Eddy Smulders, was solid, powerful, and courageous. But so was Fabrice—and on March 5, 1994, he proved it. Smulders was KO'd in the eighth round. Fabrice, the new European Middleweight Champion, had a new belt to

**Always motivated**

*Three years after losing his title, Christophe Tiozzo wants the championship belt back again. (1995)*

# FRANCE SEARCHES DESPERATELY FOR A STAR CAPABLE OF PLEASING A PUBLIC WEANED ON SUPERSTARS AND MEDIA EXCESS

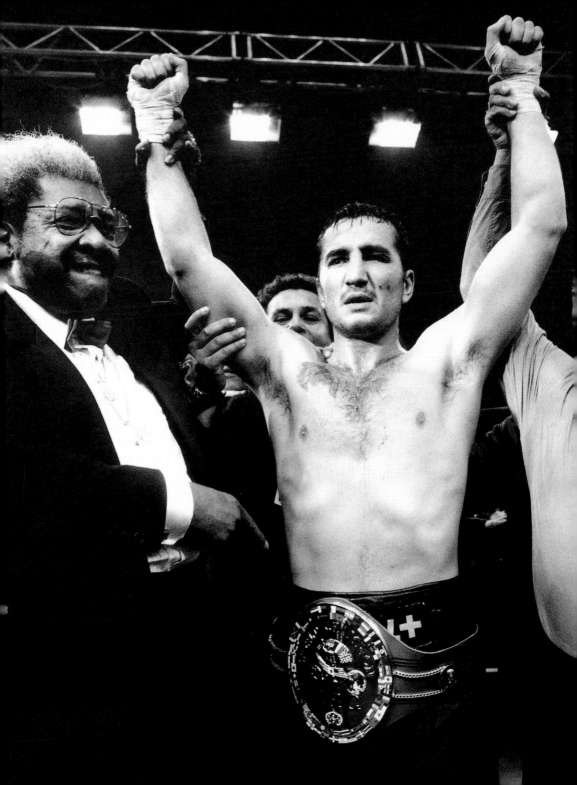

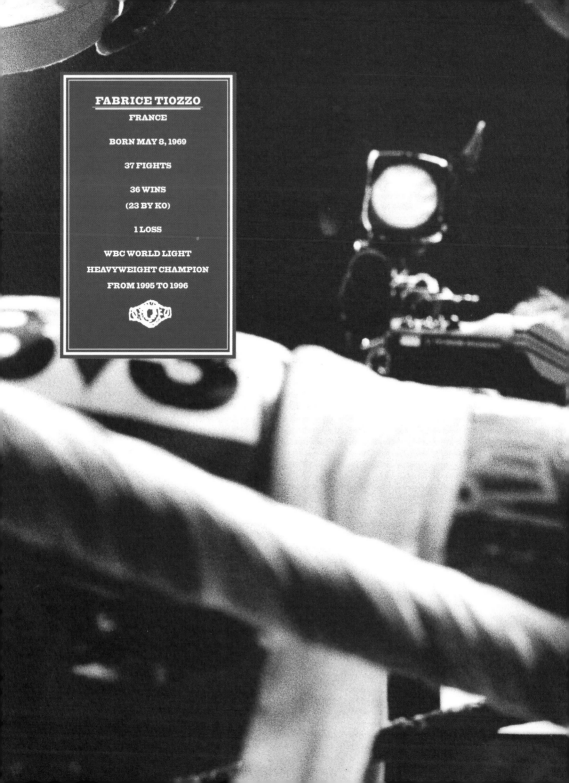

**FABRICE TIOZZO**

FRANCE

BORN MAY 8, 1969

37 FIGHTS

36 WINS
(23 BY KO)

1 LOSS

WBC WORLD LIGHT
HEAVYWEIGHT CHAMPION
FROM 1995 TO 1996

show off at the Sports Palace in Gerland. Now he knew where to find that other belt, the one that brought even more prestige and even more fame, the one that he'd already held between his hands, thanks to his brother—in Lyon, of course.

Fabrice successfully defended his title twice, against Maurice Core and Noël Magée. He and Christophe were ready to join the eleven pairs of champion brothers in the history of the Noble Art. On June 16, 1995, he challenged the man who had already beaten Jeff Harding, Christophe's nemesis of two years earlier, Mike McCallum. Talk about motivation. To prepare for the fight, Fabrice crossed gloves with Christophe, who was himself hoping to orchestrate a comeback after three years away from the ring, during which he'd spent much of his time partying. The whole Tiozzo clan was there to cheer on Fabrice. Christophe, Frank, Michffile, Robert (the father who has watched every single one of his sons' fights and hunts down any newspaper article that so much as mentions the name Tiozzo), and even Bruno (who had always been horrified by boxing). Only the boys' mother, Roberte, was missing. She refused to watch her sons "in battle" and spent the evening waiting feverishly by the telephone for news of the fight.

In a victory by decision, Fabrice won the championship title, even knocking McCallum down in the second round. The eight thousand spectators at Lyon's Sports Palace were on their feet. In the ring, the three brothers were once again united in victory.

Christophe, reliving his own fighting days, had made a decision. He wanted to be part of the glory. Now, instead of Fabrice being motivated by Christophe, it was the other way around. On October 26, 1995, at the age of thirty-one, Christophe returned to the ring and emerged victorious from his first fight in three-and-a-half years, confessing, "I needed to be back in the atmosphere of the ring." He began by beating Robert Straw, a modest American boxer, in three rounds, and then, a few months later, Carlos Norman Bates, this time in less than two rounds. But he still hadn't proved that he could become the great champion he once was. In 1996, he jumped over the next hurdle. Facing him in the ring was Philippe Michel, two-time French champion. Marcel had already had his big chance,

**SUCCESSION OF CHAMPIONS**

**(PRECEDING PAGES)** *Following in brother Christophe's footsteps, Fabrice became World Champion one June evening in 1995. The life of a champion, "just like in the pictures," opens up for him along with Frank, Jean-Claude Bouttier, and Christophe. It all happened in the blink of an eye.*

the WBO World Middleweight Championship, which he lost on points. Christophe suffered against him. He sweated, but he held on. He deserved the decision in his favor after eight rounds, if only for his courage. But something was still missing, and time was moving on. For athletes, and especially for boxers, time is the real enemy. It attacks day after day, silent, insidious, never letting go—the years were weighing on Christophe. For the first time in six years, the two brothers were on the same program. After a period of rest and relaxation following his win against McCallum, Fabrice took on the Canadian fighter, Eric Lucas, in January 1996. Fabrice won, but it wasn't a particularly convincing effort. The man who set France on fire when he won his first title was hardly recognizable. "I need a real challenge. In the middleweight division there's only one man who really motivates me, and that's Virgil Hill. Since there's no way we can meet in the ring today, I've decided to move up to cruiserweight." Fabrice confronted Leslie Stewart on a beautiful May evening in 1996. He easily took his first match in this new division, KO-ing the ex-World Middleweight Champion in the sixth round. This was his final test before going head-to-head with WBA World Cruiserweight Champion, American Nate Miller. These days, Fabrice has a double goal: he wants to become the first Frenchman to win two world titles in two different divisions.

But the fight scheduled for July 1996 never took place. And Fabrice Tiozzo lost his WBC light heavyweight title for not having defended his title during the year following his last title bout against Lucas. According to WBC rules, this was automatic grounds for losing the title. It also meant more difficulty in getting contracts and negotiating fights. Now that he was in the cruiserweight division, the WBC had made him the official challenger to the Argentinean, Dominguez. But as time went by, Fabrice was still hoping for a new chance for the world title. Sometimes it's easier to be successful than to get the right contract.

**FABRICE IS CHAMPION!**

**(PRECEDING PAGES, AND OPPOSITE)** *Against McCallum, Fabrice Tiozzo exploded under the stadium lights in Lyon. This time, the student taught "The Professor" a thing or two. The victory was a triumph for the whole Tiozzo clan, especially for Jean-Marc Perno, Fabrice's trainer, pictured here with Christophe and Frank* **(FOLLOWING PAGE)** *From the ring to the big screen—only a step separates the two from the incomparable Mickey Rourke. As for Fabrice, when will he "make the leap?"*

ROY

# jones

Champion from another dimension

"I know that no one is unbeatable. But when I look around, I don't see anyone capable of beating me." Roy Jones is certainly sure of himself. Some might even say cocky. One thing's for certain—he doesn't leave anyone indifferent. Except, maybe, his father. Roy Jones Sr. is an ex-middleweight boxer, a "journeyman," one of those boxers paid by the fight, by the day. His hour of glory had been facing Marvin Hagler in 1977. "Marvelous Marvin" was at the height of his powers and Roy Jones Sr. left the ring for good on a KO. Like father, like son. Roy Jr. inherited a sense of combat, and a desire for revenge. At the age of six, young Roy was boxing in the garage of the family home in Pensacola, Florida. His father watched, noting the talent of his son, the oldest of five children. Four years later, Roy made his competitive debut. By the age of seventeen, Roy Jr. was competing with the American team at the '88 Olympics in Korea—but with catastrophic results. Seoul turned into a nightmare for the novice boxer. He dominated his division, and in the final, facing Korean Park Si-Hun, he clearly led on points. Victory was at his fingertips, until **THE GREATEST SCANDAL IN THE HISTORY OF AMATEUR BOXING** took place. The decision was in the Korean's favor, a clear case of "home-court" favoritism. Roy Jones, robbed, disappointed, disheartened, decided to return home and take up an entirely different sport: basketball. On the court, he was no novice, and even had a certain flair for rebounding.

The young man took his time dealing with disillusionment. His father was there to help. Raised in the country, Roy Sr. had old-fashioned values. Sure that Roy Jr. would one day be champion, he also wanted to make sure his son had a good upbringing and education. During this time of emotional trial, the father's hold over the son grew stronger every day. Eight months after his disappointment in Korea, Roy Jones was back. He made his professional debut, winning with a string of KOs. In his corner, Dad was omnipresent. The "journeyman" relived his own days of glory. Maybe a little bit too much for the taste of his son, who began to find his father's presence wearisome. Before long, conflict broke out between the two generations. Roy Jr. was no longer willing to live his life within his father's tight hold. The separation was evident before the first IBF World Middleweight Championship, against Bernard Hopkins, on May 22, 1993. Roy Jones could finally let his immense strengths shine in their full glory. George Foreman called him the most exciting boxer of his time, saying **"HE HITS LIKE A HEAVYWEIGHT AND MOVES LIKE A LIGHTWEIGHT."** Boxing experts compared him to

## ROY JONES

UNITED STATES

BORN JANUARY 16, 1969

35 FIGHTS

34 WINS
(29 BY KO)
1 LOSS

IBF WORLD MIDDLEWEIGHT
CHAMPION FROM 1993 TO 1994

IBF WORLD SUPER
MIDDLEWEIGHT CHAMPION
FROM 1994 TO 1996

WBC WORLD LIGHT HEAVY-
WEIGHT CHAMPION FROM 1996

Leonard, Robinson and Ali. They claimed he had the fastest hands in boxing, lightning-quick footwork, and explosive power in both fists. It was all true, and yet Roy finished his match with nothing more exciting than a win by decision. As for Roy Sr., he was thrilled, watching the match on television. Roy Jr. hadn't forgotten what his father had done for him, or that sometimes his father did too much. After the match, his comments were double-edged: "This belt is dedicated to my father. If he has something to say, that's fine. If he doesn't, that's fine too." Roy Jones had grown up, and now he had to keep climbing. To find another challenge, he had to gain enough weight to change divisions. Among the super middleweights, one man was waiting for him. That man was James Toney, IBF World Super Middleweight Champion. After a few fights with nothing at stake, and only one title match in a year-and-a-half, Jones took the first step on a path that would lead him to the top of the pyramid. For promoter Bob Arum, there was no doubt that the fight would determine the best boxer in the world, and that it would add another name to the list of greats that already included La Motta, Cerdan, Robinson, Monzon, Hagler, and Leonard.

Admitting that Toney was a pretty decent fighter, but still sure that he couldn't be beaten, Jones made no bones about his confidence. If Detroit was a good city for boxers, Florida was the place where champions were born. As challenger, Jones arrived second in the MGM ring in Las Vegas, on November 18, 1994. He was wearing an elegant smoking jacket and a bow tie. In fact Roy Jones always transforms himself into an actor when he's in the ring. Was Toney going to put on his own show? It didn't look like it. He found himself on the ground before he knew it, in only the third round. This fight didn't promise much in the way of action. Jones was clearly the winner on points. He became known as the best boxer of his generation. McCallum, watching from the sidelines, compared Jones to Sugar Ray Robinson. **WITH EASE, ELEGANCE, SPONTANEITY, AND SPEED,** Jones flew over the ring as if it were the parquet of a basketball court. He told himself he only needed to move upwards, towards "the greats." But after a year, his record showed only fights with minor boxers like Pazienz, Thornton, and Merqui Sosa—men he'd beaten all too easily. The public was hoping for something else, a reunification of the title in a fight against the British boxer Nigel Benn. The match was constantly deferred, until it was too late. Nigel Benn lost a title match to underdog Malinga in the beginning of 1996, and along with the loss of his throne went the opportunity for what had promised to be one of the biggest matches of the decade. So what did Roy Jones really want from life? The question became important when, in 1995, he made a surprise announcement to the papers. He'd decided to become a basketball player. Stupefied and shocked, the world of pugilism didn't know what to make of this incomprehensible news. Of course, Michael Jordan, the planet-wide basketball celebrity, tried to become a baseball star before returning to his first love. Would Roy Jones do the same? Was his obsession with basketball nothing but a ploy for media attention? **JONES CALLS HIMSELF A PLAYER, A RISK-TAKER.** He tells us to have confidence in him, and to believe he's an expert at the fine art of taking the ball on the rebound.

On June 15, 1995, in Jacksonville, Florida, Roy Jones helped lead his minor league team, the Jacksonville Barracudas, to a win. Then, that very evening, there he was in the ring again, facing Canadian Eric Lucas. Roy Jones took the fight easily, maybe too easily. Still, there was no doubt that the young man who's always in search of the next big thing had won his most recent bet with himself. Next on his agenda? "Once I gain a few pounds, I'm confident of being able to beat Mike Tyson."

Does Roy Jones really believe this? He changed divisions yet again in 1996, and took the WBC Light Heavyweight title from McCallum, albeit unspectacularly. But this victory brought him a little closer to the ranks of boxing's greats, with three world titles in three different divisions. Many experts think that pound for pound he is the best boxer in the world today. But a champion of this stature has to be above reproach. And Jones was lacking in this respect against his official challenger, Montell Griffin, in March 1997. In a close fight, Jones suffered his first professional setback in the ninth round. Griffin was almost out, and was on his knees when Jones delivered the final blow. Having pushed the limits too far, Jones was disqualified.

**SWEET TALKER**

*Roy Jones is a phenomenon in the ring. His tactic?*
*"Move, hit, and talk." He has the last word here,*
*as he throws himself onto a basketball court.*

# NIGEL B

# benn

## A champion who won't give in to pain

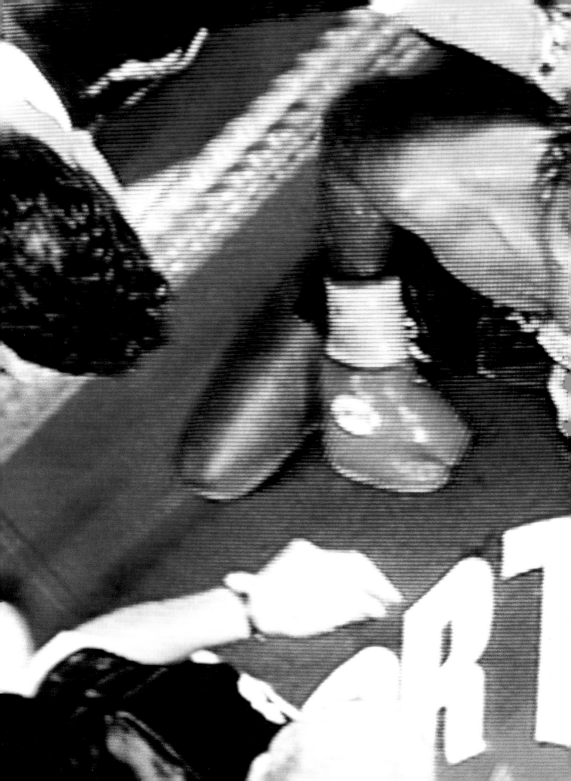

**NIGEL BENN**

**GREAT BRITAIN**

**BORN JANUARY 22, 1964**

**42 FIGHTS**

**38 WINS**

**(33 BY KO)**

**4 LOSSES**

**WBO WORLD MIDDLEWEIGHT**

**CHAMPION IN 1990**

**WBC WORLD SUPER-**

**MIDDLEWEIGHT CHAMPION**

**FROM 1992 TO 1996**

"We were at the hospital. Gerald McClellan was lying in front of me. I hugged him and kissed his hand. There was nothing else I could do, nothing else to say." Boxing can be both beautiful and tragic, inspiring emotional highs as well as lows. It can take the life of a competitor, or leave him paralyzed for life. Nigel Benn knows all of that, and he will spend the rest of his life obsessed by the memories of one fight.

On Saturday, February 25, 1995, the Englishman was defending the WBC Super Middleweight title against challenger Gerald McClellan, an American. Everyone was looking forward to a thrilling fight. Ready to give it their all, the two men were in agreement about one feeling. In the course of the evening, *someone* was going to be KO'd. No doubt about it.

Nigel Benn is used to rough fights. He still remembers the first loss of his career to fellow Englishman Michael Watson in 1989. A terrible confrontation took place that evening, and in the sixth round Benn was knocked out. Ever since that night, the name Watson has had bad associations; he is now almost completely paralyzed, the result of a fight against another Englishman, Chris Eubank. For the Benn vs. McClellan match-up, Watson had ringside seats, like at every other big fight. He was eager to watch the action now that he could no longer participate.

Chris Eubank, on the other hand, was nowhere to be seen. But Benn didn't have to see him to be thinking about him. He also hadn't forgotten his first fight against the man who would become his "intimate enemy," one November evening in 1990. It was a truly violent match, and the twelve thousand spectators in attendance were terrified by the intensity of the punches, and the power shown as the rounds continued. In the course of the fifth round, Benn's left eye closed up completely. In the eighth round, Eubank, exhausted, found himself on the ground. Finally, in the ninth round, Benn was pulled out of the fight by the referee. Eubank was victorious, but utterly exhausted. He was taken to the hospital for a medical examination. When he finally got out, several hours later, he'd regained his spirits. Fully lucid, he joked around, calling the fight a nightmare, saying he never wanted to live through such a thing again. In fact, the two men met again three years later, for a rematch in Manchester. This time, forty-eight thousand fans had come to the Old

**LOST FOREVER!**

*Gerald McClellan will soon fall into a coma,*
*following this fight against Benn (February 1996)*

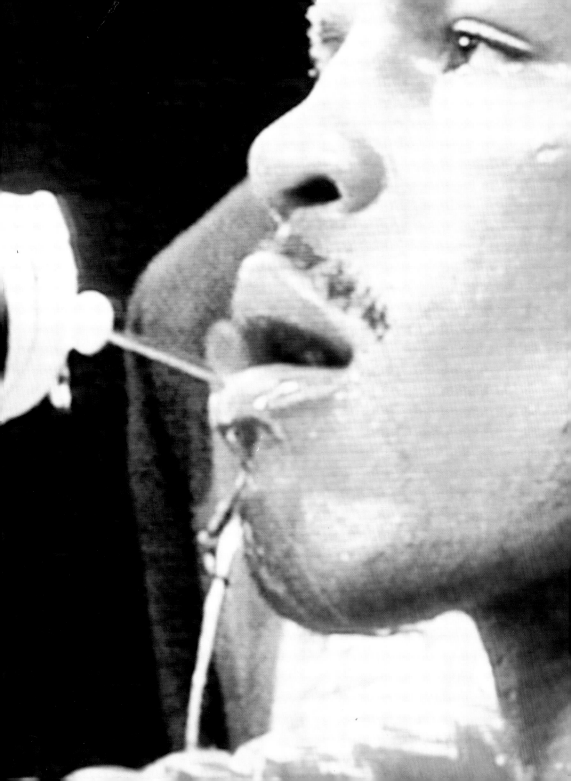

Trafford stadium, home of soccer star Eric Cantona and his Red Devils. The fight was called "The Day of Judgment," but the old intensity was missing. The boxers were holding back, and despite a few epic moments, the match ended in a draw.

But on Saturday, February 25, 1995, Nigel Benn was ready to put on his "Dark Destroyer" costume. The Destroyer, given his nickname after a string of explosive victories when he first turned pro (imagine winning by KO twenty-two times in a row!), knew that the man he was about to face was a marvel in a world of marvelous punchers. Already WBC World Middleweight Champion, McClellan had nothing to prove. His last three title defenses kept him in the ring for a grand total of two hundred and ten seconds—only as long as it took to knock out Jay Bell, Gilbert Baptist, and Julian Jackson, each time in the first round.

With the odds in his favor, despite being challenger, McClellan struck like lightning in the first thirty seconds of the match. Benn, overwhelmed, was already on the ground. The punches pelted him like hail, doubling in intensity. The American was as ferocious as the pit bulls he kept for pets at home. He even had an image of his favorite, "Deuce," tattooed on his right bicep. The fight had barely begun, and it looked like Benn had already bitten the dust. McClellan's domination was clear. But Benn, one of the most popular fighters in Great Britain, didn't want to give up in front of his home-town crowd. Full of hate and ambition, he let the storm rage around him with the kind of courage and will-power shown only by great champions—men who know how to reach deep inside themselves, to find reserves of energy and power that they never knew existed. Slowly, Benn began to come back into the fight. He was just fighting McClellan on equal ground, when, staggering with fatigue, he was surprised by a direct right. He was knocked off his feet again in the eighth round. Exit Benn? Not yet. Gathering his strength for a heroic turnaround, he destroyed his opponent's hopes with a tenth round KO.

It was a magnificent fight with a tragic conclusion. While Benn was celebrating his success, McClellan went back to his corner. He staggered there for a few seconds, and suddenly collapsed, right under the eyes of Michael Watson. The ring doctor rushed onto the scene, followed by an Emergency unit and ambulance. McClellan was in critical condition. At a nearby London hospital, McClellan was rejoined by Benn, who had a premonition of disaster while in the dressing room. He was right; the American was in serious danger. A blood clot had formed in his brain, ruining his hopes forever. No one would ever

**ONLY 30 SECONDS INTO THE MATCH, McCLELLAN MAKES LIGHTNING SPEAK!**

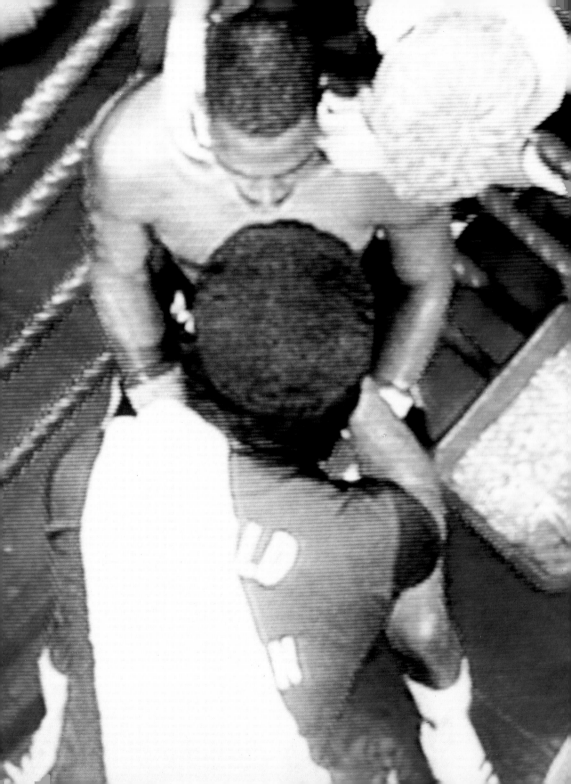

While Benn is celebrating his SUCCESS, McClellan went back to his corner. He staggerd there for a few seconds, and suddenly COLLAPSED. The ring doctor rushed onto the scene followed by an Emergency unit and ambulance. McClellan was in critical condition. A BLOOD CLOT had formed in his brain, RUINING his hopes forever. No one would ever see the powerful, courageous McClellan FIGHT AGAIN.

again see the powerful, courageous McClellan fight again. It was an ironic turn of events. McClellan, just a few years back, boasted that he was going to put Julian Jackson to sleep for a very long time. He had already KO'd Jackson twice, and predicted that the third match-up between the two men would be Julian Jackson's last fight. Boxing is spiteful, and tragic. It is for those very reasons that it is also beautiful, some would say. As for Nigel Benn, he'd been marked for life. He says he'd like to visit McClellan at his home in Michigan, but is worried about how McClellan's family would react to the man who caused their terrible tragedy. The sadness remains, a wound that will never be healed. Benn will always remember the hand that lay so still in his hand on that February evening in 1995, the hand that belonged to a champion who had lost everything.

The show must go on; but since that tragic fight, Benn hasn't been the same. It was an unconvincing victory that he won a few months later against American Danny Perez at Wembley. And once again abandoned by the motivation and self-sacrifice he had always been legendary for, he failed when facing a thirty-five-year-old veteran in March 1996. His opponent, South African Sugar Thulane Malinga, was picked to lose, at odds of four-to-one. He surprised everyone, especially Nigel Benn, who, one year after the McClellan drama, still wasn't his old fighting self. Beaten on points, Benn announced his retirement and got down on his knees in the Newcastle ring to ask the woman he loved for her hand in marriage. The "Dark Destroyer" had turned into an angel. He was almost ready to say goodbye to his past, but a few days later he came back to the ring.

In early July 1996, he confronted Steve Collins. At stake, the WBO Super-Middleweight title. But after four rounds, he suffered a sprained ankle. Benn lost a fight that ought to have made him champion once again. Four months later, however, Benn picked up the gloves and once again met Steve Collins of Scotland. And once again, he failed to go the limit, going out in the sixth round. Benn is definitely no longer the formidable warrior he was before his fight against McCallum.

**CRUCIFIED**

*No, Nigel Benn hasn't surrendered.*
*Physically and morally exhausted in an epic battle with McClellan, he wins through pain.*

JULIAN

# jackson

The greatest puncher this side of the twenty-first century

"I'm a puncher. It's true. Every time I sense my opponent within my range, just within my reach, I'm overtaken by a strange sensation, as if I were drunk...and I punch." And usually right on target, too. Nicknamed "The Falcon," he goes after his prey with diabolical precision. The slightest error, the smallest opening, and a KO is on its way. Like the one he inflicted on Isma'l Negron in only forty-six quick seconds one February evening in 1992 in Las Vegas. It was an amazing performance. In fact, it was the second-fastest KO in the history of World Middleweight Championships.

And yet Jackson's debut in 1981 wasn't particularly spectacular. He won a difficult victory by decision, after six rounds. The fighter was born in St. Thomas, capital of the Virgin Islands. It was here that Julian Jackson learned his sport. Attached to his roots, he never really wanted to leave the place that was home to some of the Carribean's most famous pirates. But before long, he had to export his budding talent to the United States. Just like another famous boxer from the Virgin Islands, three-time world champion Emile Griffith had done fifteen years earlier. Once he did leave, knockouts followed knockouts at lightning speed. Opponents found themselves clobbered, their faces against the ground—caught in mid-flight by "the Falcon."

On August 23, 1986, in Miami, Julian Jackson fought the thirtieth professional match of his career. Even more important, it was his first world championship in the Junior Middleweight division. In the opposite corner was the Jamaican Mike McCallum. McCallum, as was his habit, rocked his opponent with a thundering KO. Thrown to the ground, Jackson discovered a new sensation. He found himself in a state of grace. It was a turning point in his career, and in his life. After the loss, Jackson began to read the Bible and to live a pious life, but that year, 1986, was far from blessed for Jackson; if anything, it seemed like he'd been cursed. Accidentally injured in the right eye by a friend, Jackson didn't bother to go to a doctor. His problems worsened, and a few months later, he accidentally injured himself again—this time in the left eye. Knocked unconscious while on the beach, Jackson remained on the sand for fifteen minutes and narrowly escaped drowning.

But Julian Jackson had seen worse. Back in training, he was in top fighting form by November 21, 1987, just in time for his second Junior Middleweight World Championship. This time, he was up against In-Chul Baek. Success makes even the worst problems seem unimportant. After three rounds, the Korean was KO'd in a convincing display. The puncher from the Virgin Islands began a series of non-title matches. He also

successfully defended his championship three times. And each time, the match was over before the legal limit.

Four months after a brilliant success against Terry Norris, a second round KO on July 30, 1989, Jackson consulted Doctor Parkey, a specialist in Las Vegas. By this time, Jackson's right eye was in a terrible state; he had a detached retina, and his left eye was almost as bad. He immediately underwent operations on both eyes. Boxing receded into the past. It would be too stupid, too risky, to even think about continuing on his chosen career path. The once exceptional champion seemed to be headed towards obscurity. But six months later, Jackson pronounced himself ready to box again. He insisted that he was not going to take any foolish risks, that boxing wasn't the only important thing in his life, and he didn't want to go blind.

But there was a problem. If Jackson was sure of his health, the boxing federations and state governments had their doubts. They were not willing to take the risk of allowing Jackson into the ring. Only the WBC permitted him to fight, on November 24, 1990, against Englishman Herol Graham. Graham's World Middleweight title was at

### THUNDEROUS PUNCHES

*In the ring Julian Jackson creates a reign of terror with his devastating punch. But his career takes a turn for the worse when he meets up with Quincy Taylor. (August 1995)*

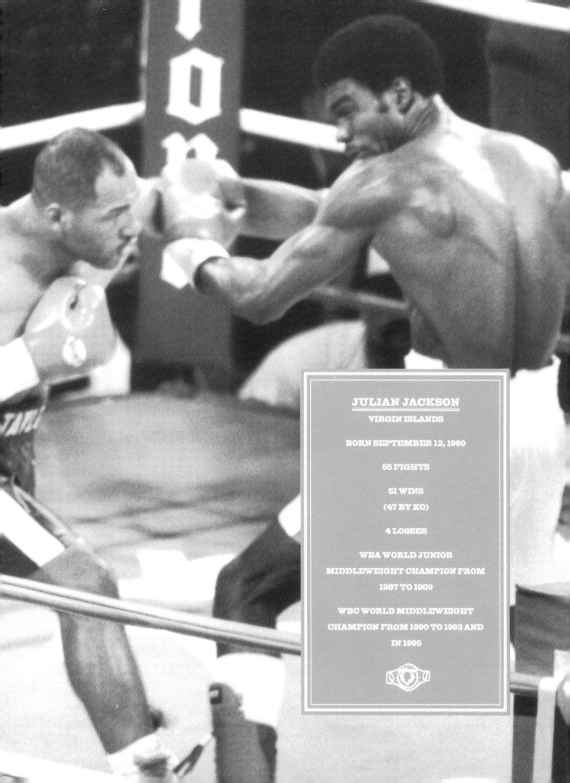

JULIAN JACKSON

VIRGIN ISLANDS

BORN SEPTEMBER 12, 1960

55 FIGHTS

51 WINS
(47 BY KO)

4 LOSSES

WBA WORLD JUNIOR
MIDDLEWEIGHT CHAMPION FROM
1987 TO 1989

WBC WORLD MIDDLEWEIGHT
CHAMPION FROM 1990 TO 1993 AND
IN 1995

stake in a fight held in a casino in Benalmadema, Spain. Nothing went right for Jackson. Before the end of the first round, his left eye was swollen shut. He staggered around the ring, like a child learning to walk, until the fourth round when he let loose with that famous right hook. Graham went down, and stayed down for five long minutes. Julian Jackson spent the time on his knees looking towards God. He was thinking about heaven, only heaven. The powerful puncher from St. Thomas had turned into a savior.

After four victorious defenses of his title, he took on another puncher, seven years his junior, on May 8, 1993. For Jackson, the fight against Gerald McClellan was more than a physical battle. He thought of the match as his last chance to prove himself. He said that if he didn't win, he would be a broken man. Jackson did lose the match, and he certainly looked broken. He fought long after he'd reached a state of exhaustion—until referee Mills Lane finally stopped him in the fifth round. Jackson was almost thirty-three years old, and it was unlikely he could come back from a defeat like this one. But he tried, one year later, in a rematch against McClellan. The fight was explosive, electrified by an emotional charge. But Jackson lost again, this time after only one minute and twenty-three seconds of fight time.

Jackson determined that it was not quite time to leave boxing behind, to go home again, to finally spend enough time with his wife Debra and the five children who idolized their famous father. The demon of the ring was always there to haunt him. How could he go home now? The middleweight throne was vacant, thanks to McClellan's decision to move up a division. Jackson had held the middleweight title for two glorious years, and still thought of it as his own. On March 17, 1995, facing the Italian Agostino Cardamone, "the Falcon" was out to prove himself. He fared ill in the first round, but unsheathed his talents in the second. Cardamone, another victim taken down in mid-flight, collapsed. Jackson was champion for the third time in his career.

Five months later, on August 18, Jackson, in his first title defense, met Quincy Taylor, fighting in his first world championship. This was to be a poisoned gift from the thirty-two-year-old Quincy, who was also a pious man in his own way, putting great faith in "his lefty star." Jackson had always feared left-handed boxers, and this fight only proved him right, forcing him finally to think about winding up his career. Taylor sent Jackson to the ground over and over again. The puncher from the Virgin Islands finished the fight on the ground, just like he had three times in his career against McCallum, and twice against

McClellan. At least his nemesis this time wasn't another "Big Mc." Just an unknown boxer, a man who until this moment had been anonymous, a fighter without a name. Well, actually he was known for one thing: he was the boxer who had never once been knocked off his feet.

At thirty-four years old, Jackson had to admit that he no longer had the punch. All that remained of "the Falcon" was a head sculpted on the handle of a cane that Jackson wouldn't let go of. He brought the cane to the ring for every fight, leaving it in a corner, like a talisman. It was as if he knew that after a certain number of blows, he would one day find himself wearing dark glasses. What good is the speed of a falcon without the eyes of an eagle?

# TERRY
# N
# norris

A passionate champion

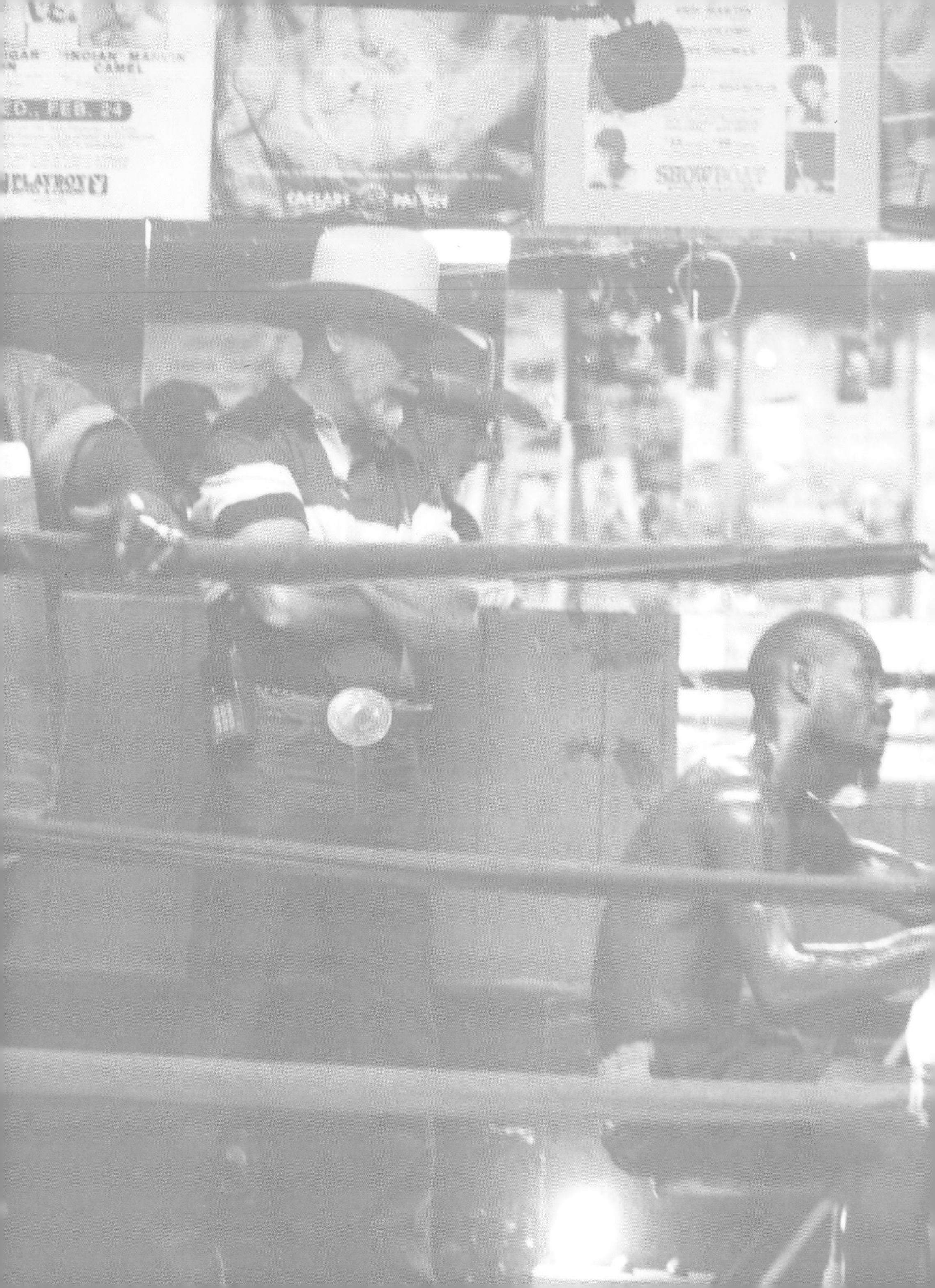
"INDIAN" MARVIN CAMEL
FEB. 24
PLAYBOY
SHOWBOAT

**STOLEN REVENGE**

*Is Norris too sure of himself before fight number two against Santana?*
*Despite the training regime of a true perfectionist, Norris will be beaten again by the Dominican.*
*And just like the first time around, he loses by disqualification.*

"It starts weeks before a fight. I don't think about anything except boxing. I sleep boxing, I eat boxing. Every day I devour my future opponent." On February 9, 1991, at the famous Madison Square Garden in New York, Terry Norris devoured a great champion. Facing him was the legendary Sugar Ray Leonard, who, at thirty-five years of age, could not withstand the ferocious energy of his young opponent. The older boxer was knocked off his feet in both the second and seventh rounds. Norris, winner by decision, pushed his illustrious predecessor, the man who had always been his idol, towards a well-deserved retirement. Only twenty-three years old, Norris already had every right to the nickname, "Terrible," which he proudly wears on the waistband of his boxing shorts. But this young man doesn't just adorn his clothing—he likes to use his own scalp as a billboard. The day of the fight he unveiled a new haircut with the letters "KO" sculpted into his hair. A new generation of boxers was born.

Norris says that what he does best is to send great boxers straight into retirement. At least

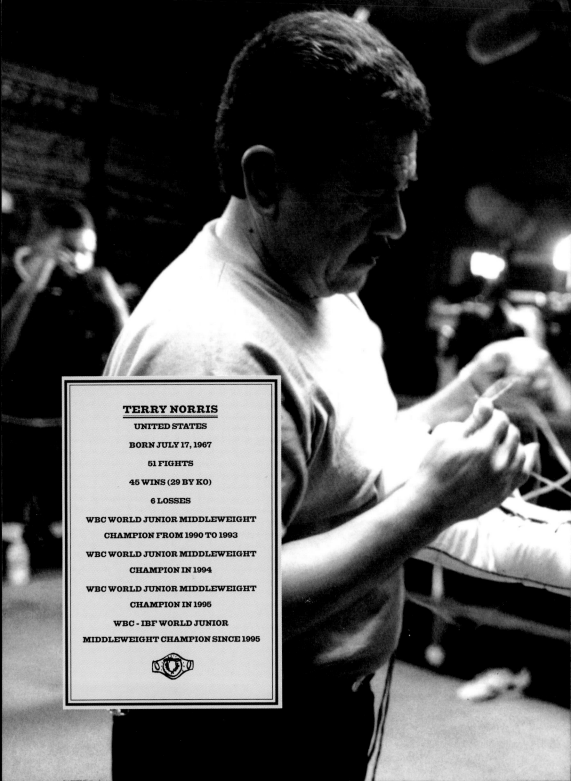

**TERRY NORRIS**

UNITED STATES

BORN JULY 17, 1967

51 FIGHTS

45 WINS (29 BY KO)

6 LOSSES

WBC WORLD JUNIOR MIDDLEWEIGHT
CHAMPION FROM 1990 TO 1993

WBC WORLD JUNIOR MIDDLEWEIGHT
CHAMPION IN 1994

WBC WORLD JUNIOR MIDDLEWEIGHT
CHAMPION IN 1995

WBC - IBF WORLD JUNIOR
MIDDLEWEIGHT CHAMPION SINCE 1995

"THE LOSS AGAINST BROWN WAS THE WORST NIGHTMARE OF MY CAREER. BUT I KNOW THAT GOD WANTED TO TEACH ME SOMETHING: TO STAY HUMBLE!"

he's open about it. And he's right. As his career took off, the numbers added up. John Mugabi, from whom he stole the Junior Middleweight title in 1990, retired as soon as he could after a terrible KO in the first round. Sugar Ray Leonard grabbed a microphone after his go-round with Norris, thanked his fans, wished young Terry the best of luck, and announced his retirement. Finally, there was Donald "the Cobra" Curry. Curry ran out of venom in 1991 against Norris, bitten in his own game in a fatal eighth round.

Terry Norris, the boxer from Lubbock, Texas, was on the scene. Many observers, including his manager, Joe Sayatovich, predicted that Norris would be the premier artist of the ring for the nineties. One of boxing's many eccentric figures, Sayatovitch never appears in public without his cowboy hat. Apparently he only takes it off to sleep, shower, and greet women. He claims that Terry has more class than all the other boxers put together, and compares his young protégé to Michael Jordan.

Only the "guru" would dare to compare his trainee with the world-wide basketball celebrity. But then Norris is the one who says defending his title is like defending his life. He proceeded to win a string of title matches, but not always against the best boxers in the division. Problems abounded: contractual difficulties, conflicts of interest among promoters, opponents who backed out at the last minute. These were opponents who were supposed to help Norris reach the next stage in his career. Norris was giving everything he had in the hopes of achieving worldwide stardom.

He was certainly a true champion, but he couldn't seem to get out of the garage and onto the open road. In fact, it's a real garage where he spends most of his time, now converted into a training gym in Campo, California. He lives the life of a recluse there, a figure straight out of the Wild West.

It was at home, along with his father and brother, ex-World Cruiserweight Champion, that he chose boxing over that other national pastime, baseball. The young man dreamed of a professional career. Then, one day in junior high school, a fellow student called Norris a crude racial epithet. The name-caller must have regretted his words when he found himself in the hospital. Hoping to channel some of the boy's excess energy, his father directed him towards boxing, the sport that he himself had practiced. It was a family affair. Young Terry's first fight, when he was fourteen, was against his brother, Orlin. He learned an important lesson early on: respect for your adversary, no matter who he is.

Terry believes in two things: hard work, and the Bible (which he carries with him everywhere in his gym bag). A huge golden cross around his neck is another testament to the boxer's faith. Before long, he was convinced of his own invincibility, successfully defending his title ten times during a forty-four-month reign as champion. Then he ran into Simon Brown. And on December 18, 1993, the hard reality of boxing hit. Norris, overconfident, was surprised, annihilated in four rounds and too many knockdowns to count.

He calls the loss against Brown his worst nightmare. But a true champion learns from every experience, even the worst ones. Norris decided that God was trying to remind him of something—to stay humble. But he forgot all too quickly, at least for the space of an evening in Puebla, Mexico. He won the rematch on points, and with class. It was a demonstration of what the "fistic" sport was meant to be.

In 1994 Norris returned to Mexico, where he had to face a challenger from the heart of the Dominican Republic, Luis Santana. Norris, dominating the match, threw a weak punch to the back of Santana's head. The blow was against the rules, but much too weak to do any harm. But Santana fell, seemingly unconscious, to the ground. Chaos ensued. He was carried off on a stretcher, and Norris was disqualified. He lost his title and Santana, the Trickster, was the winner.

Worse, Santana won the rematch by default once again. This time the fight took place in Las Vegas, on April 8, 1995. Again, Norris was dominating the match. Again, Santana, in the throes of agony, was carried off on a stretcher—this time after a right hook thrown by Norris. The punch would have been perfectly legal—if it hadn't been after the bell, which the American claimed not to have heard. In fact, Norris, hungry for revenge, fell into the trap of an average boxer with an enormous gift for acting. After three catastrophic losses, Norris' career was in free-fall. But the boxer's faith was unshakable. On August 18, 1995, in an opening match before Mike Tyson's return to the ring, Norris terrorized and ridiculed an opponent who had stolen his dreams of becoming Champion. Two rounds and a barrage of punches were too much for Santana to endure.

Twenty-eight-year-old Norris was once again WBC World Junior Middleweight Champion. He emerged victorious from his first title defense, against David Gonzales, not long after his "coronation." And then on December 16, 1995, he faced Paul Vaden, the IBF Champion of his division. Norris won the match, and was recognized as one of only two boxers in all the divisions to hold two titles at the time. Vaden was literally devoured after twelve rounds.

Since then, every fight has shown that the American is back in top form. He's won one TKO after another, against opponents, it's true, who are not up to his level. Everyone was impatiently waiting for him to take on one of the great Welterweight Champions. The final choice wasn't Whitaker or Quartey, but Trinidad. The fight was announced for the beginning of 1997. However, the legal action Norris brought a few months later against his manager, Don King, cast a shadow on the mounting drama. In the world of boxing, it seems, the more you have the more you want.

### TRICKED AGAIN

(ABOVE AND OPPOSITE) *Norris lands a punch after the bell and Santana takes full advantage.*
*He goes down and stays down. Norris the artist is disqualified once again. (April 1995)*
(PRECEDING PAGE) *"Terrible" Norris has learned his lesson.*
*Santana pays the bill only a few minutes into their third confrontation. (August 1995)*

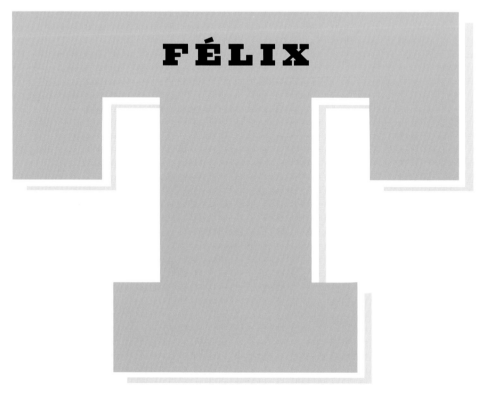

# FÉLIX

# trinidad

Teenage champion in a world of grown-up wolves

Félix Trinidad doesn't do anything like the rest of the world. With his adolescent air, you'd think he'd just graduated from some fancy liberal arts college. And you'd be right. The young Puerto Rican was a brilliant student. He was at the top of his class in the correspondence courses he took in economics at the University of San Juan. With a pedigree like that, "Baby Face" hardly seemed fit to take part in a sport for grown men, a sport without pity. Boxing at its highest level is no place for amateurs. Here, every potential champion is examined as if under a microscope, cultivated like the seed of a rare plant.

Which is exactly what happened to Félix, who, at the age of nine, was already showing a precocious passion for boxing. His obsession didn't come out of nowhere: Félix Trinidad Sr. was Puerto Rican featherweight champion in 1979. It was with his father that the young athlete went on his first morning runs, spent time in the boxing gym, and, when he was all of twelve years old, fought in his first amateur match. "Tito's" career was clearly mapped out. It was a path that led all the way to the top, to the place his father never visited, to the world of championship boxing.

Félix's qualities soon captivated boxing fans everywhere. Promoters, always on the lookout for a new star, fell over themselves trying to get an "in" with the young man. Carefully watched over by his father, he turned pro exactly two months after his seventeenth birthday. He immediately started to prove himself with a series of wins, KOs, and demonstration fights. Elegant and efficient, he soon became known outside the borders of Puerto Rico, a country that has been waiting for someone to take the place of Wilfredo Gomez and Wilfredo Benitez, both triple World Champions.

He passed his first big test in 1992, against a more experienced fighter. The fight took place in Paris, and his opponent was Argentinean Alberto Cortes. Before the fight had barely started, disaster struck. In only the second round, Trinidad found himself knocked to the ground, for the first time in his career. How would "Baby Face" react to such treatment? Did he have what it took to turn a difficult situation around? He gave the right answer in the next round, displaying his spectacular capacity for comebacks. This boxer certainly deserved to fight with the pros.

### PRECOCIOUS

*Trinidad: full speed ahead on the road to success.*
*At twenty years, five months, and nine days*
*he was already a world champion. (1995)*

**FÉLIX TRINIDAD**

PUERTO RICO

BORN OCTOBER 10, 1973

31 FIGHTS

31 WINS
(27 BY KO)

IBF WORLD WELTERWEIGHT
CHAMPION SINCE 1993

"IF I GET KNOCKED DOWN, ONLY HAVE ONE SOLUTION. GET BACK UP AGAIN AND WIPE OUT WHAT HAPPENED AS SOON A█ █ █AN."

As far as "Tito" was concerned, there's only one solution to a knockdown—to get right back up again. And then to turn around and humiliate his opponent in the same way he'd been humiliated. In Paris, his strategy was successful. Cortes was KO'd. The seed of a champion began to flower, and now he had to bloom at the world championship level. It was June 19, 1993. Trinidad was up against Maurice Blocker, and he flattened the American in only the second round. Blocker stayed down for almost twelve minutes, rising up just in time to see Trinidad brandishing the IBF World Championship belt. Twenty years, five months, and nine days old—and his future was still before him.

Trinidad returned to Puerto Rico to celebrate his victory with his family. In the ring at Bayamon, he showed that he was ready to become king in his own country. Luis Garcia, his first official challenger, was pulverized in less than one round in four trips to the ground.

Trinidad was trained by his father and managed by seventy-year-old Yamil Chade, who could have been his grandfather. Before long, he came under the influence of another important man, Don King. The famous promoter would build his career faster than anyone else could. He sent his young charge straight to the big fights. On January 29, 1994, Félix made his Las Vegas debut, as the opener for an unforgettable Chavez vs. Randall headliner match. His opponent was fellow Puerto Rican Hector Camacho, more "macho" than ever that evening. Before the fight, he called Trinidad a kid who came from nowhere, and said the youngster was still green behind the ears. Eleven years separated "Baby Face" and his opponent, who was extremely popular back home in Puerto Rico. Camacho knew what it was like to become world champion at a young age. He was only twenty-one when he won his first title. And he also knew that a defeat tonight could seal his fate. He was on guard, ready to give everything he'd got, to provoke. But it was not enough against Trinidad's budding strength. Camacho used his world class footwork to avoid losing face and being KO'd. It was the only saving grace in an evening that turned into a nightmare for the overconfident boxer. He had even bet forty thousand dollars on his own victory. But it was "Tito" who emerged victorious in the gaming capital of the world.

Trinidad remained unbeaten for twenty-three fights, until he came up against "Yori Boy" Campas. The fight took place at the now familiar MGM Las Vegas. The Mexican challenger was twenty-three years old and was also unbeaten in fifty-six fights. Although he was only two years older than Trinidad, Campas had been dreaming of a World

Championship for a long time. He had made his professional debut at the ripe old age of fifteen years and eleven months. During the second round, Trinidad hit the ground. It was the seventh time in his career that he'd found himself knocked off his feet. But he had his philosophy of perseverance to back him up. In the fourth round, Trinidad showed once again that he could take it when the going got tough. Campas was stunned by the unceasing repetition of Félix's destructive blows. Don King was beside himself. He called Trinidad a new Sugar Ray Robinson. The comparison was more than just flattering. It meant big bucks. "Tito's" entourage thought it was about time he started getting paid some real money—and not "just" four hundred thousand dollars, the purse in the fight against Campas. A rupture with Don King, who refused to pay the millions of dollars Trinidad's clan was requesting, seemed inevitable. Under contract, Trinidad fought two more times for Don King. Against Oba Carr, the scenario remained the same. Trinidad found himself on the ground, in the second round as always. He insists that the problem isn't his chin, but that he stands with his legs too close together, which makes it easy to knock him off balance. Whatever the problem is, Trinidad found a solution in round eight of the match. Once again, his punch made the decision.

Trinidad has extraordinary mental resources and will power. So much so that many were beginning to believe all the rumors about a new boxing superstar on the horizon. Trinidad lived up to the expectations. On April 8, 1995, Roger Turner was swept away in two short rounds. It was the last fight in the era of Don King; in the space of a single fight, Trinidad cut the contractual cord that had bound him to the promoter. It was time for the young boxer to try out his own wings, with his father at his side, of course, always there to guide and advise. A new emphasis on dollars didn't make Trinidad forget about the most important thing— winning. He proved it, with a win against Larry Barnes, in 1995. A KO, per usual. It was his seventh victorious IBF title defense. On the same billing, Pernell Whitaker, WBC Champion, defended his title. Present in the auditorium was Ike Quartey, WBA Champion. The "battle of the welterweights" had begun. The "Baby Face Assassin" is ready to meet these two champions, but with each promoter guarding his own interests, the fights have proved impossible to organize. So Trinidad has lined up some easy victories against second-rank opponents, hoping one day to get his big chance.

**"TRINIDAD IS A KID WHO CAME FROM NOWHERE. HE'S**

**STILL GREEN BEHIND THE EARS." HECTOR CAMACHO**

JULIO CESAR

# chavez

## Champion of a people

"I have ten brothers and sisters. We were very poor, and had to bring money home to help out. When I was very young, I sold hot dogs in parking lots and sports stadiums." Like many Mexican kids, Julio Cesar Chavez knows life in the street. But unlike some Mexican boxers who were forced into the ring by ambitious families, he chose the path that would eventually make him into a real "emperor." He is emperor for his mother, anyhow, who chose his glorious name in the first place; and "Emperor of the Noble Art" for the Mexican people, who recognize him as such. Despite his university studies, and a diploma in agricultural engineering, he chose the difficult life of the ring, because he loves to fight.

He won his first boxing match at the age of sixteen, with nothing but a beer and a sandwich for payment. Watching him were a handful of men from his hometown, Culiacan in Sinaiola, near the Gulf of California. Fourteen years later, and for a somewhat larger purse—one million dollars—he became, in the space of one February evening in 1993, a "living God" for thirty-six thousand adoring fans in Mexico's Aztec Stadium. "Chavez madness" hit Mexico like a hurricane.

Since his professional debut in 1980, Chavez has won numerous matches, taken down all sorts of opponents, chalked up a list of titles and successes that seemed to be a mile long, and, along the way, pulled his family out of the poverty into which he was born. "The bread I eat today didn't come already baked," he's fond of saying. And he shared his "bread" with some hundred and twenty people whose lives were changed by the millions of dollars won by his sweat, his hard work. Chavez is always surrounded by people—his near and extended family and friends.

Boxing requires sacrifices. Chavez knows that, as does his wife. "I want a husband. Not a champion!" she shouted at him one day in 1993, reproaches that hit as hard as one of his opponent's right hooks. Because if Chavez loves to fight, there's something else that he loves almost as well, and that's a good time. Outside the ring, the Corona flows like water at the endless parties he hosts for his friends. But the combination of slugs in the ring and slugs of beer could be a bit indigestible at times. The combination could also be inauspicious, as well as the cause of the first steps away from victory and towards failure.

After twenty-five victorious World Championships in a row, Chavez found himself in San Antonio, facing American Pernell Whitaker. A chance to add a fourth World Junior Welterweight title to the list of Lightweight and Junior Lightweight Championships he'd already won. It was September 10, 1993. Seventy thousand Texans were wearing green-

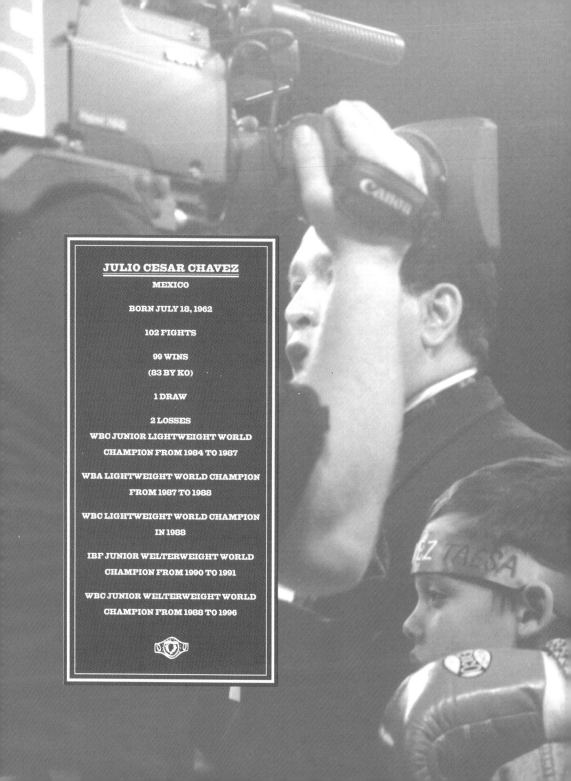

## JULIO CESAR CHAVEZ

MEXICO

BORN JULY 18, 1962

102 FIGHTS

99 WINS
(83 BY KO)

1 DRAW

2 LOSSES
WBC JUNIOR LIGHTWEIGHT WORLD
CHAMPION FROM 1984 TO 1987

WBA LIGHTWEIGHT WORLD CHAMPION
FROM 1987 TO 1988

WBC LIGHTWEIGHT WORLD CHAMPION
IN 1988

IBF JUNIOR WELTERWEIGHT WORLD
CHAMPION FROM 1990 TO 1991

WBC JUNIOR WELTERWEIGHT WORLD
CHAMPION FROM 1988 TO 1996

# "EMPEROR"
## FOR HIS MOTHER WHO CHOSE
## HIS GLORIOUS NAME,
## "EMPEROR OF THE NOBLE ART"
## FOR THE PEOPLE
## OF HIS COUNTRY:
## "CHAVEZ MANIA"
## TAKES MEXICO BY STORM!

ODAK 5063 TX 3 KODAK 5063 TX 4 KODAK 5063 TX 5 KODAK 5063

2 ⊏⇒ 2A 3 ⊏⇒ 3A 4 ⊏⇒ 4A 5 ⊏⇒ 5A

X 8 KODAK 5063 TX 9 KODAK 5063 TX 10 KODAK 5063 TX 11 KODAK 5063 TX

8 ⊏⇒ 8A 9 ⊏⇒ 9A 10 ⊏⇒ 10A 11 ⊏⇒ 11A

TX 14 KODAK 5063 TX 15 KODAK 5063 TX 16 KODAK 5063 TX 17 KODAK 5063 T

14 ⊏⇒ 14A 15 ⊏⇒ 15A 16 ⊏⇒ 16A 17 ⊏⇒ 17A

63 TX 4 KODAK 5063 TX 5 KODAK 5063 TX 6 KODAK 5063 TX 7 KODAK 50

4 ⊏⇒ 4A 5 ⊏⇒ 5A 6 ⊏⇒ 6A 7 ⊏⇒

TX 10 KODAK 5063 TX 11 KODAK 5063 TX 12 KODAK 5063 TX 13 KODAK 5

white-and-red, and waiting for a remake of the battle of the Alamo, that famous battle in 1836 when Mexican soldiers killed Davy Crockett and took the fort he was defending. Not only was Chavez trying to win his eighty-eighth fight, he was trying to do it in a new division, one where he hadn't yet boxed for a title. He was not worried. In fact, he boasted that there was only one way Whitaker could avoid humiliation—by forfeiting. But Whitaker decided to take his chances and show up for the battle. Using some fancy footwork, he fled from Chavez during the fight. He managed to avoid the Mexican's blows, even returning some of them, punch for punch. More than that, some people thought he won. The decision was a draw. For the first time in his professional career, Chavez wasn't leaving the ring clearly victorious. At the Alamo, the sounds of revolt had sounded. Was Chavez still unbeatable? The years spent in the ring were beginning to weigh on the shoulders of the WBC Junior Welterweight Champion. Nevertheless, the odds were in his favor, fifteen to one, when he faced his official challenger, Frankie Randall, on January 29, 1994. At the new MGM Las Vegas, the biggest hotel in the world, a myth crumbled in the eleventh round. Chavez had never been knocked down, not once in his whole career. But there he was, on the ground. The fall was even harder when the final verdict came in. Randall won by decision. Chavez had lost, for the first time in his life. He tried taking a historical perspective when he thought about this new turn of events: "The Berlin Wall came down. Why not Chavez?"

In fact, he had lost his passion for the sport he had once loved. It had seemed like the victories were rolling in of their own accord. With only eighteen days of training behind him, he had assumed he'd be able to win another one. Chavez wanted to erase the memory of this slap-in-the-face as soon as possible, and began listening to his wife. His entourage was sliced in half, down to twenty-five people instead of fifty. And, once again in top form, Chavez met Randall for a rematch on May 7, 1994. His clan crowed that Chavez was once again a veritable machine of destruction. They said nothing less than a superman could stop him. Their double boasts were right on target, until Chavez was stopped by an involuntary head-butt from Randall. A cut on his right eyebrow was the result, and the match had to be decided on points. Two judges to one, Chavez won, and regained his world title. But scandal was in the air at the MGM, and Randall was beside himself with rage. Boxing isn't always as clean and honest as its promoters would like to believe.

For Chavez, the important thing was that his three sons, Julio Cesar Jr., Omar and

Eduardo, could look at their father and see a hero. The "Emperor" lived up to his name once again. Not only had he regained his old glory, the "old" boxer had a new goal. Chavez decided he wanted to win one hundred fights before he retired. How will he celebrate if he reaches his aim? With a nice icy cold glass of beer, of course. In the shade, at home, in his palatial Culiacan residence. Or perhaps at the Julio Cesar Palace Hotel which he plans to build in Cancun for the modest sum of one hundred million dollars.

In the meantime, Chavez has to make the hundred fight mark. With that in mind, he met a new challenge on June 7, 1996. At stake was the biggest purse in his career: nine million dollars to meet the new boxing sensation, Oscar De la Hoya, at Caesar's Palace in Las Vegas. This fight, known as "Supreme Glory," was as much a trap as a challenge. For the first time in years, Chavez wasn't favored in the pre-fight odds. This didn't seem to worry him, but, in fact, he had a surprise on the horizon. In only four rounds, the young American reached new heights in his world championship form. Chavez's left eyebrow was open by the end of the first round, and finally the referee was obliged to stop the "massacre." It had been his thirty-fourth world championship defense, a record that beats all boxers in every division. And never, until that moment, had he been unable to finish a fight. "The Emperor" had lost his throne. But after reigning over the junior middleweight division for seven years, he was not ready to give up the title that felt so much like his personal property. He immediately called for a rematch. But will that be possible? The ten-year age difference between the two men may herald a new era. The Emperor doesn't want to put down his gloves, and hopes more than ever to reach one hundred victories before definitively quitting the ring. His plans are for his last fight to be against his countryman Angel Miguel Gonzalez for the WBC Junior Welterweight title, left vacant by De la Hoya after his victory over Gonzalez.

Then the time will have come to take care of Julio Cesar Jr., Omar, and Eduardo—his three sons who will never have to sell hot dogs in a parking lot, or climb into a ring in order to support their family. Unless they, too, love to fight.

## STRONG HEAD

*(PRECEDING PAGES) Gifted with mental powers tough enough for any situation, Julio Cesar Chavez is also famous for his remarkable physical prowess. One of his secret strengths? His cranium is considerably thicker than that of the average person. No wonder he can take the hardest blows without so much as blinking an eye. (April 1995)*

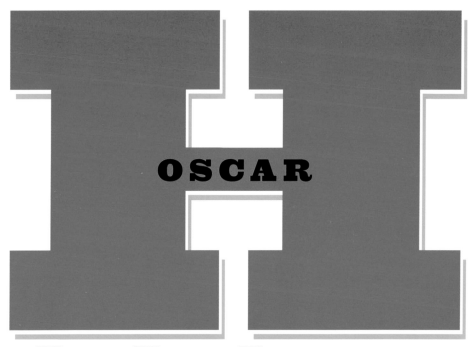

OSCAR
# de la hoya
Champion of the year 2000

**DAY OF GLORY**
*To beat Chavez on the day that marks the old champion's hundredth fight. That's the feat that
De la Hoya pulled off on June 7, 1996—a victory he'll remember for the rest of his life.*

Historically, American boxers have used the Olympic Games as a launching pad towards future glory. In 1960 Cassius Clay picked up gold in the ring in Rome. Likewise, the '68 Olympics in Mexico marked the beginning of a long and legendary career for George Foreman. In 1976, Sugar Ray Leonard gave a divine exhibition of the Sweet Science in Montreal. And 1992 was a golden year for the next American hopeful, Oscar De la Hoya. The only American boxer to win gold that year soon became known as "The Golden Boy." He was the star the world of boxing had been waiting for, ever since the artist, Sugar Ray Leonard, had retired from the ring.

At the time, De la Hoya was still a young man and had not yet recovered from the recent loss of his mother Cécilia, who had died from breast cancer just two years earlier. Up until the last days of her life, Cécilia hid her suffering from her son, not wanting to disturb the plans so carefully laid since his childhood. Oscar's first trainer, Steve Nelson, compared his

## OSCAR DE LA HOYA

UNITED STATES

BORN FEBRUARY 4, 1973

25 FIGHTS

25 WINS
(20 BY KO)

WBO JUNIOR LIGHTWEIGHT WORLD
CHAMPION IN 1994

WBO LIGHTWEIGHT WORLD
CHAMPION FROM 1994 TO 1996

IBF LIGHTWEIGHT WORLD
CHAMPION IN 1995

WBC JUNIOR WELTERWEIGHT
WORLD CHAMPION FROM 1996 TO 1997
WORLD WELTERWEIGHT CHAMPION
SINCE 1997

trainee's childhood to that of Michael Jackson. From the beginning, it was clear that the kid from East Los Angeles would make it big. With both a grandfather and a father who are ex-boxers, the life of the clearly talented young boy revolved entirely around the ring. When he became Olympic champion at Barcelona in '92, after two hundred thirty amateur fights (two hundred twenty-five wins, five losses), success was all the sweeter because of the years of hard work and sacrifice. Oscar dedicated his first big victory to his mother. After her death, he had visited her grave to make a promise. He promised that the name they shared—"De la Hoya"—would become world famous.

As an adult, Oscar gave the impression of being a well-brought-up young man: educated, intelligent, and well mannered. Unlike many other American boxers, who spent more time on the streets than in school, De la Hoya had built himself a careful reputation. He has studied to be an architect, and insists that boxing isn't going to prevent him from reaching his goal—to run his own architectural firm. In life as well in the ring, Oscar is master at the art of elegant repartee. There's no question that a new generation of stars is rising.

His talent was worth a hundred thousand dollar prize for his first pro fight. Compare that to Sugar Ray Leonard's "big" winnings—forty thousand dollars for a match at the height of his career in 1976. In November 1992, Oscar De la Hoya, in a hurry to reach the top, demolished Lamar Williams. It was the first in a series of impressive fights and quick victories.

Thirteen months after turning pro, Oscar got his first chance at a world title. He would fight for the WBO Junior Lightweight crown against Jimmy Bredhal. The match was the young American's first big test, and he passed with flying colors. Bredhal was obliged to withdraw after ten rounds. This was only De la Hoya's twelfth fight in 1994, but by the end of the year he had racked up five victorious championships, including a WBO Lightweight title. His trip to the stars continued in 1995. During the space of one year, he would meet four world or ex-world champions, one every three months. And every time, the judges could do nothing but sing his praises. John Molina pushed De la Hoya to the limit in twelve rounds; Rafael Ruelas, another young hopeful, lost his IBF Lightweight title in two quick rounds; and Genaro Hernandez completed the list of De la Hoya's victories in Las Vegas. The boxer from Los Angeles had taken the capital of betting by storm, and now he was ready for the big-time: Madison Square Garden in New York. De la

Hoya recognized the great opportunity before him: "In Las Vegas or Los Angeles, fans just want to see a fight, but here, they're waiting for real boxing. The Garden is a chance for me to grow, and to help achieve what I want for the future: to travel all over the world, and be recognized by people everywhere." Speaking both English and Spanish fluently, De la Hoya had something else to say before his first fight on the East Coast. "Frank Sinatra always said if you can make it in the Garden, you can make it anywhere." It was clear that De la Hoya was after glory.

It was December 15, 1995, almost exactly three years after the last boxing match in the legendary New York arena. Madison Square Garden could truly be called the "Mecca of boxing." The attraction this young marvel held for the pugilistic world was confirmed. In front of seventeen thousand fans, De la Hoya demolished James Leija in two rounds. Oscar called 1995 a year of learning. And what a year. *The Ring*, bible of U.S. boxing monthlies, named him "Boxer of the Year 1995." He succeeded Roy Jones (1994), Michael Carbajal (1993), Riddick Bowe (1992), James Toney (1991), and Julio Cesar Chavez (1990).

Along with Sugar Ray Leonard, Chavez had always been De la Hoya's idol. And in June of 1996, the young kid challenged the Mexican boxing emperor. To prepare himself, Oscar spent three months in a cabin designed according to his own ideas, at Big Bear, a winter sports site three hours north of Los Angeles. In the cabin, he'd tried to create the kind of ambiance his idols, the stars of the past, had lived in. A passion for architecture met a never-ending thirst for knowledge in this young man. Every minute of his spare time was spent watching videos of great boxers practicing their art: Sugar Ray Robinson, Willie Pep, José Napoles. He was searching for any little tricks of the trade he could learn from his illustrious predecessors. And when he finally stood in the ring opposite Chavez, De la Hoya's bag of tricks was pretty impressive. Champion in two different divisions, he went on to become the youngest champion to hold titles in three divisions. His third was the junior welterweight, which had belonged to the Mexican. Oscar's trainer, Robert Alcazar, insisted that anyone who doubted the boxer until this match would worship him from then on. As far as Alcazar was concerned, De la Hoya represented the beginning of a new generation. In the ring at Caesar's Palace in Las Vegas, De la Hoya was physically transformed. It was the result of a pre-fight preparation scientifically calculated to make him gain twenty percent in speed and thirty percent in power in exactly three months.

Mentally, he exhibited a calmness and serenity shocking for someone only twenty-three years old. The differences between him and the aging Chavez were stark. On June 7, 1996, a great champion was born in less than four rounds. De la Hoya had already succeeded at the first half of his bet with himself, to win six titles in six different divisions. But the young man was in a hurry to make good on the promise he had made to Cécilia, to build another kind of life for himself.

De la Hoya decided to move into the welterweight category after beating his fellow Mexican, Miguel Angel Gonzalez. On April 12, 1997, he challenged the title held by Pernell Whitaker, already quadruple World Champion. It was a difficult and close fight which De la Hoya finally won on points. But the important thing was the result: De la Hoya now had a fourth title, just like Whitaker and the Panamanian Robert Duran. And he continues to push on forward. "I'll only be in boxing for a few years more. Later, I want to devote myself to architecture." Or perhaps golf, his new passion. In just a few months he has achieved a handicap of ten. De la Hoya really is the "Golden Boy."

ALSO FEATURING THE PROFESSIONAL BOXING DEBUT OF

# "MARIELITO"
# MICKEY ROURKE
Miami, FL/Hollywood, CA
## vs.
# STEVE POWELL
Boston Mass.

# AFTERWORD

## BY MICKEY ROURKE

**Past years have seen numerous books and collections of photography about boxing.** Most of them are, by and large, unimpressive. But this book is truly insightful, and Richard's photos are most dramatic. He has succeeded in his mission to capture the soul of the sport. He has spent long and tiresome hours traveling around the world to get to know and respect this great profession, and his easy-going manner has won the trust and cooperation of these hard, complicated, and intelligent men. The old cliché that all fighters are slurred-speech brutes is ignorant and narrow-minded. In fact, it is quite the contrary. Fighters are a special breed: hard-working, dedicated, spirited, and brave.

As a young boy in Miami's Fifth Street gym, I was very privileged to have trained on the same wood as Muhammad Ali. For over five years I watched and learned many things from this man, who I believe to be the greatest professional boxer who ever lived. From my early encounters with Ali to my current friendship with Roberto Duran, I believe I have become a better person from the lessons I've learned from them. To me there is no other feeling that can compare to the electricity and fear I've experienced in the ring. **You have to be there to know it.**

# APPENDIX

## DIVISIONS

| | | | | | |
|---|---|---|---|---|---|
| STRAWWEIGHT | 105 LBS. | FEATHERWEIGHT | 126 LBS. | MIDDLEWEIGHT | 160 LBS. |
| JUNIOR FLYWEIGHT | 108 LBS. | JUNIOR LIGHTWEIGHT | 130 LBS. | SUPER MIDDLEWEIGHT | 168 LBS. |
| FLYWEIGHT | 112 LBS. | LIGHTWEIGHT | 135 LBS. | LIGHT HEAVYWEIGHT | 175 LBS. |
| JUNIOR BANTAMWEIGHT | 115 LBS. | JUNIOR WELTERWEIGHT | 140 LBS. | CRUISERWEIGHT | 190 LBS. |
| BANTAMWEIGHT | 118 LBS. | WELTERWEIGHT | 147 LBS. | HEAVYWEIGHTWEIGHT | UNL. |
| JUNIOR FEATHERWEIGHT | 122 LBS. | JUNIOR MIDDLEWEIGHT | 154 LBS. | | |

The weights above indicate the upper limit for each division. A boxer who weighs more than 105 lbs. up to and including 108 lbs. would be a Junior Flyweight. More than 175 lbs. up to and including 190 lbs. would be Cruiserweight. Boxers must be within the limit for their division on the day of the pre-fight weigh-in.

## FEDERATIONS

| | | | | |
|---|---|---|---|---|
| **IBF** | · | INTERNATIONAL BOXING FEDERATION | **WBC** | WORLD BOXING COUNCIL |
| **WBA** | | WORLD BOXING ASSOCIATION | **WBO** | WORLD BOXING ORGANIZATION |

# INDEX OF FIGHTS

tko: *technical KO*     W: *win against*     L: *loss against*     D: *draw*     TD: *technical draw*     dis: *disqualified*

## MIKE TYSON

**WBC HEAVYWEIGHT**
| 11/22/86 | Las Vegas W *Trevor Berbick* | tko 2 |

**WBA-WBC HEAVYWEIGHT**
| 03/07/87 | Las Vegas W *James Smith* | 12 |
| 05/30/87 | Las Vegas W *Pinklon Thomas* | tko 6 |

**WBA-WBC-IBF HEAVYWEIGHT**
| 08/01/87 | Las Vegas W *Tony Tucker* | 12 |
| 10/16/87 | Atlantic City W *Tyrell Biggs* | tko 7 |
| 01/22/88 | Atlantic City W *Larry Holmes* | tko 4 |
| 03/21/88 | Tokyo W *Tony Tubbs* | tko 2 |
| 06/27/88 | Atlantic City W *Michael Spinks* | ko 1 |
| 02/25/89 | Las Vegas W *Frank Bruno* | tko 5 |
| 07/21/89 | Atlantic City W *Carl Williams* | tko 1 |
| 02/11/90 | Tokyo L *James Douglas* | ko 10 |

**WBC HEAVYWEIGHT**
| 03/16/96 | Las Vegas W *Frank Bruno* | tko 3 |

**WBA HEAVYWEIGHT**
| 09/07/96 | Las Vegas W *Bruce Seldon* | ko 1 |
| 11/09/96 | Las Vegas L *Evander Holyfield* | tko 11 |
| 06/28/97 | Las Vegas L *Evander Holyfield* | dis 3 |

## GEORGE FOREMAN

**HEAVYWEIGHT**
| 01/22/73 | Kingston W *Joe Frazier* | ko 2 |
| 09/01/73 | Tokyo W *José Roman* | ko 1 |
| 03/25/74 | Caracas W *Ken Norton* | tko 2 |
| 10/30/74 | Kinshasa L *Muhammad Ali* | tko 8 |
| 04/19/91 | Atlantic City L *Evander Holyfield* | 12 |

**WBO HEAVYWEIGHT**
| 06/07/93 | Las Vegas L *Tommy Morrison* | 12 |

**WBA-IBF HEAVYWEIGHT**
| 11/05/94 | Las Vegas W *Michael Moorer* | ko 12 |

**IBF HEAVYWEIGHT**
| 04/22/95 | Las Vegas W *Axel Schulz* | 12 |

## EVANDER HOLYFIELD

**WBA CRUISERWEIGHT**
| 07/12/86 | Atlanta W *Muhammad Qawi* | 15 |
| 02/14/87 | Reno W *Henry Tillman* | tko 7 |

**WBA-IBF CRUISERWEIGHT**
| 05/15/87 | Las Vegas W *Ricky Parkey* | tko 3 |
| 08/15/87 | Saint-Tropez W *Osvaldo Ocasio* | tko 11 |
| 12/05/87 | Atlantic City *Muhammad Qawi* | ko 4 |

**WBA-WBC-IBF CRUISERWEIGHT**
| 04/09/88 | Las Vegas W *Carlos de Leon* | tko 8 |

**WBA-WBC-IBF HEAVYWEIGHT**
| 10/25/90 | Las Vegas W *James Douglas* | tko 4 |
| 04/19/91 | Atlantic City W *George Foreman* | 12 |
| 11/23/91 | Atlanta W *Bert Cooper* tko | 7 |
| 06/19/92 | Las Vegas W *Larry Holmes* | 12 |
| 11/13/92 | Las Vegas L *Riddick Bowe* | 12 |

**WBA-IBF HEAVYWEIGHT**
| 11/06/93 | Las Vegas W *Riddick Bowe* | 12 |
| 04/22/94 | Las Vegas L *Michael Moorer* | 12 |

**WBA HEAVYWEIGHT**
| 11/09/96 | Las Vegas W *Mike Tyson* | tko 11 |
| 06/28/96 | Las Vegas W *Mike Tyson* | dis 3 |

## RIDDICK BOWE

**WBA-WBC-IBF HEAVYWEIGHT**
| 11/13/92 | Las Vegas W *Evander Holyfield* | 12 |

**WBA-IBF HEAVYWEIGHT**
| 02/06/93 | New York W *Michael Dokes* | tko 1 |
| 05/22/93 | Washington W *Jesse Ferguson* | ko 2 |
| 11/06/93 | Las Vegas L *Evander Holyfield* | 12 |

**WBO HEAVYWEIGHT**
| 03/11/95 | Las Vegas W *Herbie Hide* | tko 6 |
| 06/17/95 | Las Vegas W *Jorge Gonzales* | ko 6 |

## BRUCE SELDON

**WBA HEAVYWEIGHT**
| 04/08/95 | Las Vegas W *Tony Tucker* | tko 7 |
| 08/19/95 | Las Vegas W *Joe Hipp* | tko 8 |
| 09/07/96 | Las Vegas L *Mike Tyson* | ko 1 |

## LARRY HOLMES

**WBC HEAVYWEIGHT**
| 06/09/78 | Las Vegas W *Ken Norton* | 15 |
| 11/10/78 | Las Vegas W *Alfredo Evangelista* | ko 7 |
| 03/23/79 | Las Vegas W *Osvaldo Ocasio* | ko 7 |
| 06/22/79 | New York W *Mike Weaver* | tko 11 |
| 09/28/79 | Las Vegas W *Earnie Shavers* | tko 11 |
| 02/03/80 | Las Vegas W *Lorenzo Zanon* | tko 6 |
| 03/31/80 | Las Vegas W *Leroy Jones* | tko 8 |
| 07/07/80 | Bloomington W *Alan Scott Leloux* | tko 7 |
| 10/02/80 | Las Vegas W *Muhammad Ali* | tko 11 |

| | | | |
|---|---|---|---|
| 04/11/81 | Las Vegas W *Trevor Berbick* | | 15 |
| 06/12/81 | Detroit W *Leon Spinks* | | tko 3 |

### WBO HEAVYWEIGHT

| | | | |
|---|---|---|---|
| 11/07/81 | Pittsburg W *Renaldo Snipes* | | tko 11 |
| 06/11/82 | Las Vegas W *Gerry Cooney* | | tko 13 |
| 11/26/82 | Houston W *Randall Tex Cobb* | | 15 |
| 03/27/83 | Scranton W *Lucien Rodriguez* | | 12 |
| 05/20/83 | Las Vegas W *Tim Witherspoon* | | 12 |
| 09/10/83 | Atlantic City W *Scott Frank* | | tko 5 |
| 11/25/83 | Las Vegas W *Marvin Frazier* | | tko 1 |

### IBF HEAVYWEIGHT

| | | | |
|---|---|---|---|
| 11/09/84 | Las Vegas W *James Smith* | | tko 12 |
| 03/15/85 | Las Vegas W *David Bey* | | tko 10 |
| 05/20/85 | Reno W *Carl Williams* | | 15 |
| 09/21/85 | Las Vegas L *Michael Spinks* | | 15 |
| 04/19/86 | Las Vegas L *Michael Spinks* | | 15 |

### WBA-WBC-IBF HEAVYWEIGHT

| | | | |
|---|---|---|---|
| 01/22/88 | Las Vegas L *Mike Tyson* | | tko 4 |
| 06/19/92 | Las Vegas L *Evander Holyfield* | | 12 |
| 04/08/95 | Las Vegas L *Oliver McCall* | | 12 |

## LENNOX LEWIS

### WBC HEAVYWEIGHT

| | | | |
|---|---|---|---|
| 05/08/93 | Las Vegas W *Tony Tucker* | | 12 |
| 10/1/93 | Cardiff W *Frank Bruno* | | tko 7 |
| 05/06/94 | Atlantic City W *Phil Jackson* | | ko 8 |
| 09/24/94 | London L *Oliver McCall* | | ko 2 |
| 02/08/97 | Las Vegas W *Oliver McCall* | | tko 5 |

## OLIVER McCALL

### WBC HEAVYWEIGHT

| | | | |
|---|---|---|---|
| 09/24/94 | London W *Lennox Lewis* | | ko 2 |
| 05/08/95 | Las Vegas W *Larry Holmes* | | 12 |
| 09/24/95 | London L *Frank Bruno* | | 12 |
| 02/08/97 | Las Vegas L *Lennox Lewis* | | tko 5 |

## MIKE McCALLUM

### WBA JUNIOR MIDDLEWEIGHT

| | | | |
|---|---|---|---|
| 10/19/84 | New York W *Sean Mannion* | | 15 |
| 12/01/84 | Milan W *Luigi Minchillo* | | tko 14 |
| 07/28/85 | Miami W *David Braxton* | | ko 8 |
| 08/23/85 | Miami W *Julian Jackson* | | tko 2 |
| 10/25/85 | Paris W *Said Skouma* | | ko 9 |
| 04/19/87 | Phoenix W *Milton McCrory* | | tko 10 |
| 07/18/87 | Las Vegas W *Donald Curry* | | ko 5 |

### WBA MIDDLEWEIGHT

| | | | |
|---|---|---|---|
| 03/05/88 | Pesaro L *Sumbu Kalambay* | | 12 |

| | | | |
|---|---|---|---|
| 05/10/89 | London W *Herol Graham* | | 12 |
| 02/03/90 | Boston W *Steve Collins* | | 12 |
| 04/14/90 | London W *Michael Watson* | | tko 11 |
| 04/01/91 | Monte Carlo W *Sumbu Kalambay* | | 12 |

### IBF MIDDLEWEIGHT

| | | | |
|---|---|---|---|
| 12/13/91 | Atlantic City D *James Toney* | | 12 |
| 08/00/92 | Reno L *James Toney* | | 12 |

### WBC LIGHT HEAVYWEIGHT

| | | | |
|---|---|---|---|
| 07/23/94 | Faroo W *Jeff Harding* | | 12 |
| 02/25/95 | London W *Karl Jones* | | tko 7 |
| 06/16/95 | Lyon L *Fabrice Tiozzo* | | 12 |
| 11/22/96 | Tampa L *Roy Jones* | | 12 |

## FABRICE TIOZZO

### WBA LIGHT HEAVYWEIGHT

| | | | |
|---|---|---|---|
| 04/03/93 | Levallois L *Virgil Hill* | | 12 |

### WBC LIGHT HEAVYWEIGHT

| | | | |
|---|---|---|---|
| 06/16/95 | Lyon W *Mike McCallum* | | 12 |
| 01/13/96 | Saint-Etienne W *Eric Lucas* | | 12 |

## CHRISTOPHE TIOZZO

### WBA SUPER MIDDLEWEIGHT

| | | | |
|---|---|---|---|
| 03/30/90 | Lyon W *In-Chul Baek* | | tko 7 |
| 07/20/90 | Arles W *Paul Whitaker* | | tko 8 |
| 11/23/90 | Cergy W *Danny Morgan* | | tko 2 |
| 04/05/91 | Marseille L *Victor Cordoba* | | tko 9 |

### WBC LIGHT HEAVYWEIGHT

| | | | |
|---|---|---|---|
| 06/05/92 | Marseille L *Jeff Harding* | | tko 8 |

## ROY JONES

### IBF MIDDLEWEIGHT

| | | | |
|---|---|---|---|
| 05/22/93 | Washington W *Bernard Hopkins* | | 12 |
| 05/27/94 | Las Vegas W *Thomas Tate* | | tko 2 |

### IBF SUPER MIDDLEWEIGHT

| | | | |
|---|---|---|---|
| 11/18/94 | Las Vegas W *James Toney* | | 12 |
| 03/18/95 | Pensacola W *Antoine Byrd* | | tko 1 |
| 06/24/95 | Atlantic City W *Vinnie Pazienza* | | tko 6 |
| 09/20/95 | Pensacola W *Tony Thornton* | | tko 3 |
| 06/15/96 | Jacksonville W *Eric Lucas* | | ko 11 |

### WBC LIGHT HEAVYWEIGHT

| | | | |
|---|---|---|---|
| 11/22/96 | Tampa W *Mike McCallum* | | 12 |
| 03/22/97 | Atlantic City L *Montell Griffin* | | Dis 9 |

## NIGEL BENN

### WBO MIDDLEWEIGHT

| | | | |
|---|---|---|---|
| 04/29/90 | Atlantic City W *Doug De Witt* | | tko 8 |
| 08/18/90 | Las Vegas W *Iran Barkley* | | tko 1 |
| 11/18/90 | Birmingham L *Chris Eubank* | | tko 9 |

WBC Super Middleweight

| | | |
|---|---|---|
| 10/03/92 | Marino W *Mauro Galvano* | tko 4 |
| 12/12/92 | London W *Nicky Piper* | tko 11 |
| 03/06/93 | Glasgow W *Mauro Galvano* | 12 |
| 06/26/93 | Earls Court W *Lou Gent* | tko 4 |
| 10/09/93 | Manchester D *Chris Eubian* | ko 12 |
| 02/26/94 | London W *Henry Wharton* | 12 |
| 09/10/94 | Birmingham W *Juan Gimenez* | 2 |
| 02/25/95 | London W *Gerald McClellan* | ko 10 |
| 07/22/95 | London W *Vincenzo Nardiello* | tko 8 |
| 03/09/96 | Newcastle L *Thulane Malinga* | 12 |
| 07/??/96 | UK L *Steve Collinskot* | 4 |
| 11/09/96 | Manchester L *Steve Collinskot* | 6 |

## JULIAN JACKSON

WBA Junior Middleweight

| | | |
|---|---|---|
| 08/23/86 | Miami L *Mike McCallum* | tko 2 |
| 11/21/87 | Las Vegas W *In-Chul Back* | tko 3 |
| 07/29/88 | Atlantic City W *Buster Drayton* | ko 3 |
| 02/25/89 | Las Vegas W *Franco De Jesus* | ko 8 |
| 07/30/89 | Atlantic City W *Terry Norris* | tko 2 |

WBC Middleweight

| | | |
|---|---|---|
| 11/24/90 | Benalmadena W *Herol Graham* | ko 4 |
| 09/14/91 | Las Vegas W *Dennis Milton* | ko 1 |
| 02/15/92 | Las Vegas W *Ismael Negron* | ko 1 |
| 04/10/92 | Mexico W *Ron Collins* | tko 5 |
| 08/01/92 | Las Vegas W *Thomas Tate* | 12 |
| 05/08/93 | Las Vegas L *Gerald McClellan* | tko 5 |
| 05/07/94 | Las Vegas L *Gerald McClellan* | tko 1 |
| 03/17/95 | Las Vegas W *Agostino Cardamone* | tko 2 |
| 08/19/95 | Las Vegas L *Quincy Taylor* | tko 5 |

## TERRY NORRIS

WBA Junior Middleweight

| | | |
|---|---|---|
| 07/30/89 | Atlantic City L *Julian Jackson* | tko 2 |

WBC Junior Middleweight

| | | |
|---|---|---|
| 03/31/90 | Tampa W *John Mugabi* | ko 1 |
| 07/13/90 | Annecy W *René Jacquot* | 12 |
| 02/09/91 | New York W *Ray Leonard* | 12 |
| 06/01/91 | Palm Springs W *Donald Curry* | tko 8 |
| 08/17/91 | San Diego W *Brett Lally* | ko 1 |
| 12/13/91 | Paris W *Jorge Castro* | 12 |
| 02/22/92 | San Diego W *Carl Daniels* | tko 9 |
| 05/09/92 | Las Vegas W *Meldrick Taylor* | tko 4 |
| 02/20/93 | Mexico W *Maurice Blocker* | tko 2 |
| 06/19/93 | San Diego W *Troy Waters* | tko 3 |
| 09/10/93 | San Antonio W *Joe Gatti* | ko 1 |

| | | |
|---|---|---|
| 12/04/93 | Puebla L *Simon Brown* | ko 4 |
| 05/07/94 | Las Vegas W *Simon Brown* | 12 |
| 12/11/94 | Mexico L *Luis Santana* dis | 5 |
| 04/08/95 | Las Vegas L *Luis Santana* dis | 3 |
| 08/19/95 | Las Vegas W *Luis Santana* | tko 2 |
| 09/16/95 | Las Vegas W *David Gonzalez* tko | 9 |

WBC-IBF Junior Middleweight

| | | |
|---|---|---|
| 12/16/95 | Philadelphia W *Paul Vaden* | 12 |
| 01/27/96 | Phoenix W *Jorge Luis Valdo* | ko 2 |
| 02/24/96 | Richmond W *Vincent Pettway* | ko 9 |
| 09/07/96 | Las Vegas W *Alex Rios* | tko 5 |
| 01/11/97 | Nashville W *Nick Rupa* | tko 10 |

## FÉLIX TRINIDAD

IBF Welterweight

| | | |
|---|---|---|
| 06/19/93 | San Diego W *Maurice Blocker* | ko 2 |
| 08/06/93 | Bayamon W *Luis Garcia* | tko 1 |
| 10/23/93 | Fort Lauderdale W *Anthony Stephens* | ko 10 |
| 01/29/94 | Las Vegas W *Hector Camacho* | 12 |
| 09/17/94 | Las Vegas W *Luis Ramon Campas* | tko 4 |
| 12/10/94 | Monterrey W *Oba Carr* | tko 8 |
| 04/08/95 | Las Vegas W *Roger Turner* | ko 2 |
| 11/18/95 | Atlantic City W *Larry Barnes* | tko 4 |
| 02/10/96 | Las Vegas W *Rodney Moore* | tko 4 |
| 05/18/96 | Las Vegas W *Freddie Pendleton* | ko 5 |
| 09/07/96 | Las Vegas W *Ray Lovato* | tko 6 |
| 01/11/97 | Nashville W *Kevin Lueshing* | tko 3 |

## JULIO CESAR CHAVEZ

WBC Junior Lightweight

| | | |
|---|---|---|
| 09/13/84 | Los Angeles W *Mario Martinez* | ko 8 |
| 04/19/85 | Los Angeles W *Ruben Castillo* | ko 6 |
| 07/07/85 | Las Vegas W *Roger Mayweather* | tko 2 |
| 09/21/85 | Las Vegas W *Dwight Pratchett* | 12 |
| 03/22/86 | Paris W *Faustino Barrios* | tko 5 |
| 06/13/86 | New York W *Refugio Rojas* | tko 7 |
| 08/03/86 | Monte Carlo W *Rocky Lockridge* | 12 |
| 12/12/86 | New York W *Juan La Porte* | 12 |
| 04/18/87 | Nimes W *Francisco Tomas Da Cruz* | tko 3 |
| 08/21/87 | Tijuana W *Danilo Cabrera* | 12 |

WBA Lightweight

| | | |
|---|---|---|
| 11/21/87 | Las Vegas W *Edwin Rosario* | tko 11 |
| 04/16/88 | Las Vegas W *Rodolfo Aguilar* | tko 6 |

WBA-WBC Lightweight

| | | |
|---|---|---|
| 10/29/88 | Las Vegas W *José Luis Ramirez* | 11 |

WBC Junior Welterweight

| | | |
|---|---|---|
| 05/13/89 | Inglewood W *Roger Mayweather* | ko 10 |

| | | |
|---|---|---|
| 11/18/89 | Las Vegas W *Sammy Fuentes* | rko 10 |
| 12/16/89 | Mexico W *Alberto Cortes* | tko 3 |

### WBC-IBF Junior Welterweight

| | | |
|---|---|---|
| 03/17/90 | Las Vegas W *Meldrick Taylor* | rko 12 |
| 12/08/90 | Atlantic City W *Kyung-Duk Ahn* | tko 3 |

### WBC Junior Welterweight

| | | |
|---|---|---|
| 03/18/91 | Las Vegas W *John Duplessis* | tko 4 |
| 09/14/91 | Las Vegas W *Lonnie Smith* | 12 |
| 04/10/92 | Mexico W *Angel Hernandez* | tko 5 |
| 08/01/92 | Las Vegas W *Frank Mitchel* | tko 4 |
| 09/12/92 | Las Vegas W *Hector Camacho* | 12 |
| 02/20/93 | Mexico W *Greg Haugen* | tko 5 |
| 05/08/93 | Las Vegas W *Terrence Alli* | tko 6 |
| 09/10/93 | San Antonio D *Pernell Whitaker* | 12 |

| | | |
|---|---|---|
| 12/18/93 | Puebla W *Andy Holligan* | tko 5 |
| 01/29/94 | Las Vegas L *Frankie Randall* | 12 |
| 05/07/94 | Las Vegas W *Frankie Randall* | tw 8 |
| 09/17/93 | Las Vegas W *Meldrick Taylor* | tko 8 |
| 12/10/94 | Monterrey W *Tony Lopez* | tko 10 |
| 04/08/95 | Las Vegas W *Giovanni Parisi* | 12 |
| 09/16/95 | Las Vegas W *David Kamau* | 12 |
| 06/07/96 | Las Vegas L *Oscar De la Hoya* | tko 4 |

### OSCAR DE LA HOYA

#### WBC Junior Lightweight

| | | |
|---|---|---|
| 01/18/97 | Las Vegas W *Miguel Angel Gonzalez* | 12 |
| 04/12/97 | Las Vegas W *Pernell Whitaker* | 12 |
| 06/14/97 | San Antonio W *David Kamau* | ko 2 |

# RECORDS:
# WORLD TITLES IN MORE
# THAN ONE DIVISION

## 5 Titles

**Sugar Ray Leonard, U.S.**
1979  Welter *(WBC, unified in 1981)*
1981  Junior Middleweight *(WBA)*
1987  Middleweight *(WBC)*
1988  Super Middleweight *(WBC)*
1988  Light Heavyweight *(WBC)*

**Thomas Hearns, U.S.**
1980  Welterweight *(WBA)*
1982  Junior Middleweight *(WBC)*
1987  Light Heavyweight *(WBC, WBA in 1991)*
1987  Middleweight *(WBC)*
1988  Super Middleweight *(WBO)*

## 4 Titles

**Oscar De la Hoya, U.S.**
1994  Junior Lightweight *(WBO)*
1994  Lightweight *(WBO)*
1996  Jr Welterweight (WBC)
1997  Welterweight (WBC)

**Pernell Whitaker, U.S.**
1989  Lightweight *(IBF, IBF-WBC, Unified in 1990)*
1992  Junior Welterweight *(IBF)*
1993  Welterweight *(WBC)*
1995  Junior Middleweight *(WBA)*

**Roberto Duran, Panama**
1972  Lightweight *(WBA, Unified in 1978)*
1980  Welterweight *(WBC)*
1983  Junior Middleweight *(WBA)*
1989  Middleweight *(WBC)*

## 3 Titles

**Alexis Arguello, Nicaragua**
1974  Flyweight *(WBA)*
1978  Junior Lightweight *(WBC)*
1981  Lightweight *(WBC)*

**Henry Armstrong, U.S.**
1937  Flyweight
1938  Welterweight and
Lightweight

**Iran Barkley, U.S.**
1988  Middleweight *(WBC)*
1992  Super Middleweight *(IBF)*
1992  Light Heavyweight *(WBA))*

**Wilfred Benitez, Puerto Rico**
1976  Junior Welterweight *(WBA)*
1979  Welterweight *(WBC)*
1981  Junior Middleweight *(WBC)*

**Hector Camacho, Puerto Rico**
1983  Junior Lightweight *(WBC)*
1985  Lightweight *(WBC)*
1989  Junior Welterweight *(WBO)*

**Tony Canzoneri, U.S.**
1928  Featherweight
1930  Lightweight
1931  Junior Welterweight

**Julio Cesar Chavez, Mexico**
1984  Junior Lightweight *(WBC)*
1987  Lightweight *(WBA, WBA-WBC in 1988)*
1988  Junior Welterweight *(WBC, WBC-IBF in 1990)*

**Jeff Fenech, Australia**
1985  Bantamweight *(IBF)*
1987  Junior Featherweight *(WBC)*
1988  Featherweight *(WBC)*

**Bob Fitzsimmons, U.S.**
1891  Middleweight
1897  Heavyweight
1903  Light Heavyweight

**Wilfredo Gomez, Puerto Rico**
1977  Junior Featherweight *(WBC)*
1984  Featherweight *(WBC)*
1985  Junior Lightweight *(WBA)*

**Roy Jones, U.S.**
1993  Middleweight *(IBF)*
1994  Super Middleweight *(IBF)*
1996  Light Heavyweight (WBC)

Mike McCallum, U.S.
1984   Junior Middleweight *(WBC)*
1989   Middleweight *(WBA)*
1994   Light Heavyweight *(WBC)*
Duke McKenzie, U.K.
1988   Flyweight *(IBF)*
1991   Bantamweight *(WBO)*
1992   Junior Featherweight *(WBO)*
Daniel Zaragoza, Mexico
1985   Bantamweight *(WBC)*
1988   Junior Featherweight *(WBC)*
1995   Featherweight *(WBC)*

## 2 Titles

Benny Bass, U.S.
1927   Flyweight
1929   Junior Lightweight
Nigel Benn, U.K.
1990   Middleweight *(WBO)*
1992   Super Middleweight *(WBC)*
Nino Benvenuti, Italy
1965   Junior Middleweight
1967   Middleweight
Lou Brouillard, Canada
1932   Welterweight
1933   Middleweight
Simon Brown, U.S.
1988   Welterweight *(IBF, IBF-WBC in 1991)*
1993   Junior Middleweight *(WBC)*
Freddie Castillo, Mexico
1978   Junior Flyweight
1982   Flyweight
Bobby Chacon, U.S.
1974   Flyweight
1982   Junior Welterweight
Kid Chocolate, U.S.
1931   Junior Lightweight
1932   Featherweight
Jum-Choi, Korea
1986   Junior Flyweight
1990   Strawweight
Donald Curry, U.S.
1983   Welterweight
1988   Junior Middleweight
Bobby Czyz, U.S.

1986   Light Heavyweight *(IBF)*
1991   Cruiserweight *(WBA)*
George Dixon, U.S.
1890   Bantamweight
1891   Featherweight
Johnny Dundee, U.S.
1921   Junior Lightweight
1922   Featherweight
Louie Espinoza, U.S.
1987   Junior Featherweight *(WBA)*
1989   Featherweight *(WBO)*
Chris Eubank, U.K.
1990   Middleweight *(WBO)*
1991   Super Middleweight *(WBO)*
Joey Gamache, U.S.
1991   Junior Lightweight *(WBA)*
1992   Lightweight *(WBA)*
Silvio Gamez, Venezuela
1988   Strawweight *WBA)*
1993   Junior Flyweight *WBA)*
Emile Griffith, U.S.
1961   Welterweight
1966   Middleweight
Mashiko Harada, Japan
1962   Flyweight
1965   Bantamweight
Greg Haugen, U.S.
1986   Lightweight *(IBF)*
1991   Junior Welterweight *(WBO)*
Evander Holyfield, U.S.
1986   Cruiserweight *(WBA, IBF in 1987, unified in 1988)*
1990   Heavyweight *(unified, WBA-IBF in 1993)*
Soo-Hwan Hong, Korea
1974   Bantamweight *(WBA)*
1977   Junior Featherweight *(WBA)*
Hiroki Ioka, Japan
1987   Strawweight *(WBC)*
1991   Junior Flyweight *(WBA)*
John David Jackson, U.S.
1988   Junior Middleweight *(WBO)*
1993   Middleweight *(WBA)*
Julian Jackson, U.S.
1987   Junior Middleweight *(WBA)*
1990   Middleweight *(WBC)*

Hary Jeffra, U.S.
1937   Bantamweight
1940   Featherweight
Eder Jofre, Brazil
1962   Bantamweight
1973   Featherweight *(WBC)*
Muangchai Kittikasem, Thailand
1989   Junior Flyweight *(IBF)*
1991   Flyweight *(WBC)*
Yul-Woo Lee, Korea
1989   Junior Lightweight *(WBC)*
1990   Featherweight *(WBA)*
Tony Lopez, U.S.
1988   Junior Lightweight *(IBF)*
1992   Lightweight *(WBA)*
Roger Mayweather, U.S.
1983   Junior Lightweight *(WBA)*
1987   Junior Welterweight *(WBC)*
James McGirt, U.S.
1988   Junior Welterweight *(IBF)*
1991   Welterweight *(WBC)*
Terry McGovern, U.S.
1899   Bantamweight
1900   Featherweight
Kennedy McKinney, U.S.
1992   Junior Featherweight *(IBF)*
1996   Junior Featherweight *(WBO)*
Dariusz Michalczewski, Germany
1994   Light Heavyweight *(WBO)*
1994   Cruiserweight *(WBO)*
Sung-Kil Moon, Korea
1988   Bantamweight *(WBA)*
1990   Junior Flyweight *(WBC)*
Michael Moorer, U.S.
1988   Light Heavyweight *(WBO)*
1992   Heavyweight *(WBO, WBA-IBF in 1994)*
Azumah Nelson, Ghana
1984   Featherweight *(WBC)*
1988   Junior Lightweight *(WBC)*
Michael Nunn, U.S.
1988   Middleweight *(IBF)*
1992   Super Middleweight *(WBA)*
Ruben Olivares, Mexico
1969   Bantamweight
1974   Featherweight

Carlos Ortiz, Puerto Rico
1959   Junior Welterweight
1962   Lightweight
Giovanni Parisi, Italy
1992   Lightweight (WBO)
1996   Junior Welterweight (WBO)
Tracy Harris Patterson, U.S.
1992   Junior Featherweight (WBC)
1995   Junior Lightweight (IBF)
Vinnie Pazienza, U.S.
1987   Lightweight (IBF)
1991   Junior Middleweight (WBA)
Diosdato Penalosa, Philippines
1983   Junior Flyweight (IBF)
1987   Flyweight (IBF)
Raul Perez, Mexico
1988   Bantamweight (WBC)
1991   Junior Featherweight (WBA)
Bernardo Pinango, Venezuela
1986   Bantamweight (WBA)
1988   Junior Featherweight
        (WBA)

Lupe Pintor, Mexico
1979   Bantamweight (WBC)
1985   Junior Featherweight (WBC)
Dwight Muhammad Qawi, U.S.
1981   Light Heavyweight (WBC)
1985   Cruiserweight (WBA)
Sugar Ray Robinson, U.S.
1946   Welterweight
1951   Middleweight
Edwin Rosario, Puerto Rico
1983   Lightweight (WBC, WBA in 1986)
1991   Junior Welterweight (WBA)
Tommy Ryan, U.S.
1894   Welterweight
1898   Middleweight
Kuniaki Shibata, Japan
1970   Featherweight (WBC)
1973   Junior Lightweight (WBA)
Michael Spinks, U.S.
1981   Light Heavyweight (WBA,
        unified in 1983)
1985   Heavyweight (IBF)

Meldrick Taylor, U.S.
1988   Junior Welterweight (IBF)
1991   Welterweight (WBA)
Dick Tiger, Nigeria
1963   Middleweight
1966   Light Heavyweight
James Toney, U.S.
1991   Middleweight (IBF)
1993   Super Middleweight (IBF)
Darrin Van Horn, U.S.
1989   Junior Middleweight (IBF)
1991   Super Middleweight (IBF)
Wilfredo Vasquez, Puerto Rico
1987   Bantamweight (WBA)
1992   Junior Featherweight (WBA)
Hilario Zapata, Panama
1980   Junior Flyweight (WBC)
1985   Flyweight (WBA)

# CHAMPIONS...
# OF WORLD CHAMPIONSHIPS

*Thirty-nine boxers have won at least fifteen world championships during their careers.*
*At the head of the list is the "Emperor," Julio Cesar Chavez!*
(*boxer is still active)

### 34 CHAMPIONSHIPS

JULIO CESAR CHAVEZ, MEXICO*
Junior Lightweight, Lightweight, Junior
Welterweight, Welterweight
*31 wins, 1 draw, 2 losses, 1984 to 1996*

### 27 CHAMPIONSHIPS

JOE LOUIS, U.S.
Heavyweight
*26 wins, 1 loss, 1937 to 1950*

### 26 CHAMPIONSHIPS

HENRY ARMSTRONG, U.S.
Featherweight, Welterweight, Lightweight,
Middleweight
*22 wins, 1 draw, 3 losses, 1937 to 1941*

LARRY HOLMES, U.S.*
Heavyweight
*22 wins, 5 losses*

### 25 CHAMPIONSHIPS

MUHAMMAD ALI, U.S.
Heavyweight
*22 wins, 3 losses, 1964 to 1980*

### 24 CHAMPIONSHIPS

AZUMAH NELSON, GHANA*
Featherweight, Junior Lightweight,
Lightweight
*18 wins, 2 draws, 4 losses, 1982 to 1996*

### 23 CHAMPIONSHIPS

WILFREDO GOMEZ, PUERTO RICO
Junior Featherweight, Featherweight,
Junior Lightweight
*20 wins, 3 losses, 1977 to 1986*

VIRGIL HILL, U.S.*
Light Heavyweight
*22 wins, 1 loss, 1987 to 1996*

MANUEL ORTIZ, U.S.
Bantamweight
*21 wins, 2 losses, 1942 to 1950*

HILARIO ZAPATA, PANAMA
Junior Flyweight, Flyweight
*18 wins, 1 draw, 4 losses, 1980 to 1987*

## 22 CHAMPIONSHIPS

ALEXIS ARGUELLO, NICARAGUA
Featherweight, Junior Lightweight,
Lightweight, Junior Welterweight
*19 wins, 3 losses, 1974 to 1983*

TONY CANZONERI, U.S.
Bantamweight, Featherweight, Lightweight,
Junior Welterweight
*12 wins, 1 draw, 9 losses, 1927 to 1937*

GEORGE DIXON, U.S.
Bantamweight, Featherweight
*18 wins, 2 draws, 2 losses, 1890 to 1900*

EMILE GRIFFITH, U.S.
Welterweight, Junior Middleweight,
Middleweight
*14 wins, 8 losses, 1961 to 1976*

TERRY NORRIS, U.S.*
Junior Middleweight
*18 wins, 4 losses, 1989 to 1991*

EUSEBIO PEDROZA, PANAMA
Bantamweight, Featherweight
*19 wins, 1 draw, 2 losses, 1976 to 1985*

SUGAR RAY ROBINSON, U.S.
Welterweight, Middleweight, Light
Heavyweight
*14 wins, 1 draw, 7 losses*

PERNELL WHITAKER, U.S.*
Lightweight, Junior Welterweight,
Welterweight, Junior Middleweight
*19 wins, 1 draw, 2 losses, 1988 to 1997*

## 21 CHAMPIONSHIPS

ANTONIO CERVANTES, COLUMBIA
Junior Welterweight
*18 wins, 3 losses, 1971 to 1980*

ROBERTO DURAN, PANAMA
Lightweight, Welterweight, Junior
Middleweight, Middleweight, Super
Middleweight
*16 wins, 5 losses from 1972 to 1989*

MYUNG-WOO YUH, KOREA
Junior Flyweight
*20 wins, 1 loss, 1985 to 1993 (abandoned
his title)*

## 20 CHAMPIONSHIPS

KAOSA· GALAXY, THAILAND
Junior Bantamweight
*20 wins, 1984 to 1991 (abandoned his title)*

## 19 CHAMPIONSHIPS

JUNG-KOO CHANG, KOREA
Junior Flyweight
*16 wins, 3 losses, 1982 to 1990*

THOMAS HEARNS, U.S.*
Welterweight, Junior Middleweight,
Middleweight, Super Middleweight,
Light Heavyweight
*14 wins, 1 draw, 4 losses, 1980 to 1992*

## 18 CHAMPIONSHIPS

MIGUEL CANTO, MEXICO
Flyweight
*15 wins, 1 draw, 2 losses, 1973 to 1979*

MIKE MCCALLUM, JAMAICA*
Junior Middleweight, Middleweight,
Super Middleweight, Light Heavyweight
*13 wins, 1 draw, 4 losses, 1984 to 1996*

JOSE NAPOLES, CUBA
Welterweight, Middleweight
*15 wins, 3 losses, 1969 to 1975*

CARLOS ORTIZ, PUERTO RICO
Junior Welterweight, Lightweight
*14 wins, 4 losses, 1959 to 1968*

GIANFRANCO ROSI, ITALY*
Junior Middleweight
*14 wins, 1 draw, 2 losses, 1 no-contest,
1987 to 1995*

SAM SERRANO, PUERTO RICO
Junior Lightweight
*15 wins, 1 draw, 2 losses, 1976 to 1983*

## 17 CHAMPIONSHIPS

BETULIO GONZALEZ, VENEZUELA
Flyweight
*7 wins, 2 draws, 8 losses*

DANIEL ZARAGOZA, MEXICO*
Bantamweight, Junior Featherweight,
Featherweight
*10 wins, 3 draws, 4 losses, 1985 to 1995*

## 16 CHAMPIONSHIPS

CARLOS DE LEON, PUERTO RICO
Cruiserweight
*11 wins, 1 draw, 4 losses, 1980 to 1990*

GILBERTO ROMAN, MEXICO
Junior Bantamweight
*12 wins, 1 draw, 3 losses, 1986 to 1990*

## 15 CHAMPIONSHIPS

GABRIEL ELORDE, PHILIPPINES
Flyweight, Junior Lightweight, Lightweight
*11 wins, 4 losses*

YOKO GUSHIKEN, JAPAN
Junior Flyweight
*14 wins, 1 loss, 1976 to 1981*

MARVIN HAGLER, U.S.
Middleweight
*13 wins, 1 draw, 1 loss, 1979 to 1987*

CARLOS MONZON, ARGENTINA
Middleweight
*15 wins, 1970 to 1977 (abandoned his title)*

MICHAEL SPINKS, U.S.
Light Heavyweight, Heavyweight
*14 wins, 1 loss, 1981 to 1988*

**RICHARD AUJARD** is a sports photographer. For three years, he traveled regularly to Las Vegas, getting first-hand experience in the world of boxing, and taking the photos for this book. His work has appeared in numerous magazines, including *Max*, *Vogue Homme*, *Paris-Match*, *Photo*, *VSD*, *Esquire*, and *Sky*. Currently, he is working on a feature film, *A Question of Honor*, about the world of boxing. Starring in the film are the Tiozzo brothers, Mickey Rourke, Lydia Andre, Marcel Cerdan Jr., Stéphane Ferrara, Jean-Claude Bouttier, and the Cantona brothers.

*He would like to dedicate this book*
*to César and Lydia.*

**CHRISTIAN DELCOURT** has been a reporter for the major French television station, *Canal+*, since 1989. Along with Jean-Claude Bouttier, he has provided cable television commentary for all the major fights of the last decade. Through the years, Delcourt has become a trusted interviewer and a good friend to most of the world champions presented in this book.

**ACKNOWLEDGEMENTS :** *Our grateful thanks to the Boxing service at Canal+, Jean-Claude Bouttier and Olivier Cocatrix, to Mickael Marley, Don King, Franck Tiozzo, Jean-Marc Perono, Jérôme Valcke, Zora Moktari and Marc Dolisi, Sam Djob, and to the Monocle Studio.*

**PHOTOGRAPHY CREDITS :** p. 23, © Keystone; p. 35, © Agence Vu; pp. 20, 24, 25, 26, 27, 29 and 32 © Allsport/Jed Jacobson; All rights reserved. All other photographs © Richard Aujard.